Horoscopes of Africa

Marc Penfield

ISBN-10: 0-86690-591-X
ISBN-13: 978-0-86690-591-6

Cover Design: Jack Cipolla

Published by:
American Federation of Astrologers, Inc.
6535 S. Rural Road
Tempe, AZ 85283

www.astrologers.com

Printed in the United States of America

This book is dedicated to DAVID & FEI COCHRANE
for the computer and to
KRIS BRANDT RISKE
my editor who always
makes me look good in print

Contents

Introduction

This book is my sixth and final book on countries of the world arranged by continent. In some ways it was the easiest to compile as most of the countries were "born at midnight" and references regarding their births were recorded in numerous newspapers. However, as I had done no previous research on Africa, I had to start from scratch and double-check all facts from numerous sources which took more time than I had anticipated.

As noted in my previous books, I began my research into mundane, or geopolitical, astrology in the early 1970s while employed as a cataloguer and bibliographer for an antiquarian bookstore in southern California. Unlike other books I've written on the continents, I could not rely on personal experience for Africa as I did with Europe, Asia or Australia. One of these days I would dearly love to journey to this continent and visit South Africa, Kenya and especially Egypt.

At the beginning of the 20th century, there were only two countries in Africa that could have been called as such, Ethiopia and Liberia. The rest were colonies of European powers like Great Britain, France, Spain, Portugal, Belgium or Germany. By the outbreak of World War I, the nation of South Africa had been born, and by the end of World War II, movements for independence began to surface for self-rule and autonomous government. During the early 1950s, Egypt and Libya threw off the yoke of imperialism, and by the end of that decade a few other countries had been hatched.

The big push, however, occurred during the 1960s when 32 nations were born; 17 of them were born during 1960. Eight more were founded in the 1970s, but only two more during the following decade. The youngest nations in Africa are Namibia (formerly Southwest Africa, (ruled by South Africa) and Eritrea, a former Italian colony that was also once a province of Ethiopia. Fourteen countries were born under the sign of Cancer, a region that the ancient astrologer Ptolemy, thought ruled this part of the world. Ten countries are under the sign of Leo but only one is ruled by Aquarius. There is only one colony remaining in Africa, Western Sahara, which is currently administered by Morocco.

The modern chart for Ethiopia is for the moment when Emperor Haile Selassie was told "to get out of town" and his reign was terminated. Technically, by modern standards, Liberia is the oldest nation in Africa, having been founded in July 1847 by the American Colonization Society.

The sources for most of the birthtimes and birthdates come from newspapers like the *New York Times*, *Los Angeles Times* and the *Times* of London. I also wish to thank Nicholas Campion for his excellent tome, *The Book of World Horoscopes*. Besides the above-listed newspapers, he also had access to papers not microfilmed at our local library. A few nations have moved their capitals since independence, so if you wish to relocate the specific charts, please feel free to do so. Otherwise, despite the fact that most African countries were born at midnight, various time-zone accuracy was extremely important, especially in the case of Mauretania.

Charts for the cities of Africa are speculative as to the time of day with the exception of Cairo and Johannesburg which had accurately recorded moments of inception. When it was necessary to use a charter or incorporation date, that time was presumed to be at midnight. I wish I had been able to get the founding dates for all African cities, but like Asia, some of those places were founded in antiquity and only an approximation could be made.

Africa is the second-largest continent on earth and with an area of 11.5 million square miles has 20 percent of the earth's land mass. Its population of 900 million, with 15 percent of the world's inhabitants, is second only to Asia. Nigeria and Egypt are the most-populous countries; the most-sparscly populated is Namibia, while Uganda has the youngest overall population. Africa has eight out of 10 of the most fertile nations on Earth: the highest birth rate is in Niger where the rate is over four times that of the United States.

Madagascar is the world's fourth-largest island, slightly smaller than Texas. Africa also has the world's longest river, the Nile, which runs from Lake Victoria to the Mediterranean, a distance of 4145 miles. This continent also has the world's third-largest body of water, Lake Victoria (the size of West Virginia) and its second-deepest inland body of water, Lake Tanganyika, exceeded only by Lake Baikal in Russia. Africa also has the third-longest canal, the Suez, which runs for 103 miles from the Mediterranean to the Red Sea. Africa also has some of the largest reservoirs on earth; Lake Nasser behind the Aswan High Dam in Egypt being the most famous. The greatest natural geological feature of this continent is the Great Rift Valley which runs from Jordan across the Red Sea into Ethiopia then down the eastern side of Africa where it splits in two, one section ending in Botswana, the other around Lake Nyasa in Mozambique.

Africa has the world's largest desert, the Sahara, which encompasses about one-third of the continent, the size of the US or Brazil. The highest point is Mt. Kilimanjaro (19,340 ft.) and the tallest volcano is Mt. Cameroon (13,435 ft.) Africa also has 17 of the world's 20 poorest nations, as well as 3.5 million refugees.

Africa's infant mortality rate is appalling: in Sierra Leone the rate is 165 per 1000 births. In America, the rate is seven, still higher than in most countries of western Europe. Life expectancy is low as well: 33 years in Swaziland and only slightly higher in Botswana and Lesotho. The highest rate is in Tunisia and Libya. In some countries, the rate is falling due to epidemics and warfare, not to mention AIDS, which is endemic in sub-Saharan Africa.

I sincerely hope that by reading this book you will be motivated to buy my other books on the continents with their countries' horoscopes. If you have any additions or suggestions, please write to the publisher.

Marc Penfield
July 2008

Planets, Houses and Aspects in Mundane Astrology

Planets

Sun—Governs the will of the people and their inherent characteristics. Rules all political activities and persons in power and authority.

Moon—Rules the common people, their personality and desire for change. Also has dominion over the basic necessities of life such as food, clothing and shelter.

Mercury—Rules the people's ability and desire to communicate as well as their literary interests and desire for movement and travel.

Venus—Represents the people's desire to make their community more attractive. It governs high society, the arts and culture.

Mars—Governs the energy of the people. It has dominion over manufacturing and industrial concerns. It also rules the police and the military.

Jupiter—Governs the religious and moral principles of a people and their capacity for law and order. It also illustrates the desire to elevate themselves financially or spiritually.

Saturn—Governs conservatism and right-wing elements of society. It also shows the ability to accomplish desired goals and degree of ambition. It also shows the restrictive elements which must be overcome lest ruin and disgrace tarnish the reputation of the community.

Uranus—Has dominion over radical and progressive elements and all left-wing activities. Uranus rules riots, rebellions and all acts which upset the status quo and equilibrium of the community.

Neptune—Governs the ideals of the people as well as their desire to communicate with outsiders. Neptune governs the mass media, all chain stores and places which are franchised. It also governs problems relating to alcoholism, drug addiction and mental diseases.

Pluto—Represents the group effort and degree of cooperation that is to be expected to accomplish a desired goal. Pluto rules transformations, such as urban renewal mergers, foreign alliances and treaties, especially if those relate to finance or trade.

Houses

First—Represents the people and the first impression one gets when viewing a particular place as well as the disposition, temperament and personality of the people. This house acts as a lens through which the rest of the horoscope is filtered.

Second—Represents the people's attitudes towards material possessions and their sense of values. It shows their potential wealth and assets and all places were earnings and investments are deposited.

Third—Illustrates the people's ability and desire to communicate. Governs the postal service, the mass media and all forms of transportation and literary interests. Also rules elementary education (K-12).

Fourth—Shows the people's desire for security and ownership of real estate. Governs houses, apartment houses and condos, permanent or transient. Also governs agriculture, farmers and miners. Also has a great deal to do with weather and climate patterns.

Fifth—Shows the people's ability to amuse themselves. Governs theatres, cinemas, gambling halls as well as prostitution. Governs the stock market and other forms of speculation as well as children.

Sixth—Represents the workers of the community or country, especially those in the employ of the government. All civil service workers, police and military come under its jurisdiction. Also governs health concerns.

Seventh—Governs the people's ability to relate to outsiders and their desire to form alliances or treaties. Failure to balance and adjust might result in conflict and could lead to war. Also governs tourism.

Eighth—Shows the debts of the people and their taxation. Also rules insurance companies and credit card firms. This house also illustrates which areas need to be regenerated or destroyed in order for the entire structure to perform at maximum efficiency.

Ninth—Shows the people's desire for law and order. Governs the courts and the church and all forms of higher education such as colleges or universities. All international concerns and commercial interests come under the dominion of the ninth house.

Tenth—Represents the leader of the people, be it their president or prime minister, king or dictator, their mayor or governor. Also shows the people's attitude towards those in power and authority and the general reputation of the community. This house also shows the outcome of elections and referendums.

Eleventh—Represents the friends, allies, supporters and backers of the community. It governs legislators, congressmen, senators and aldermen. Also shows the general philanthropy and bequests to a community.

Twelfth—Illustrates the hidden ills of the community. Hospitals, asylums, jails and prisons as well as those who work in these institutions come under this house's dominion. Those on welfare and support from SSI or unemployment insurance are shown here as well.

Aspects

Aspects can be hard or soft, what we used to call benefic or malefic. They often indicate specific static conditions (soft) or clarifying obstacles with which one must eventually cope (hard).

Conjunction ($0°$)—Neither hard nor soft, depending upon the nature of the planets conjoined. This aspect blends varying elements into a single unit: Venus conjunct Jupiter is easier than Mars conjunct Saturn, for example.

Semisquare ($45°$)—Mildly irritating and vexing, like a rash that won't go away because you won't keep from scratching it.

Sextile (60°)—Offers numerous opportunities through social contacts that can be highly beneficial. It's mildly lucky but also energetic.

Square (90°)—Indicates obstacles which must be overcome and the areas of life that need the most improvement and attention. Highly energetic but also frustrating.

Trine (120°)—Indicates a harmonious state of being and potential for luck but in itself is passive and lacking in energy. Keeps the status quo.

Sesquare (135°)—Indicates frustration and annoyance often with mental anomalies which will require patience and calm.

Inconjunct or Quincunx (150°)—Like mixing oil and vinegar between two forces that will never really mix as they have nothing in common. This is the "fly in the ointment" or "monkey wrench" aspect which requires considerable adjustment or compromise in order to function at all.

Opposition (180°)—Indicates literal opposition in temperament or methodology that exists between two forces which are reluctant to blend that could lead eventually to either cooperation or conflict.

Algeria

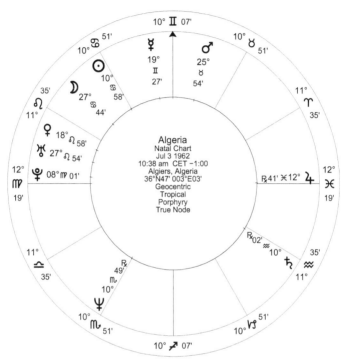

July 3, 1962, 10:38 a.m. MET, Algiers
Sources: *New York Herald Tribune*; **also, New Y***ork Times* **says**
10:07 a.m., and *Le Monde* **from Paris says 10:30 a.m.**

Algeria was first settled by Phoenicians around 1200 B.C. Then came the Carthaginians and finally the Romans in the 2nd century B.C. The Arabs invaded in 640 A.D., bringing Islam. The Ottomans took over in 1518. The French made Algeria their first African possession in 1830, long a stronghold for the Barbary pirates.

Independence from France came in July 1962 after a years-long struggle for freedom. Ahmed Ben Bella ruled from 1963 to 1965, but was ousted when a coup installed Houari Boumedienne (progressed MC semisquare Moon square Jupiter, progressed Sun semisquare Uranus).

The Islamic Salvation Front (FIS) won the election in 1991 but the opposing party (FLN) cancelled the results and declared a state of emergency (progressed MC sextile Pluto). A terrorist campaign transpired from 1992 to 1999.

An offshoot of Al-Qaida in North Africa claimed responsibility for numerous strikes in teh country throughout 2007. More than 116 people were killed in grenade attacks and car bombings (progressed Ascendant semisquare Pluto).

Algeria is the second-largest country in Africa in size, some three times the area of Turkey. Its 33 million people are 65 percent Arab and 35 percent Berber, most of which live in a region called the Tell, a strip 75 miles wide along the south coast of the Mediterranean. The south part contains the Atlas Mountains, and 80 percent of Algeria lies within the Sahara. The coastline is 620 miles long. Oil and gas make up 90 percent of its exports.

Algiers

Algiers was founded around 1200 B.C. by the Phoenicians on four islands. They called the place Icosium. It was refounded in 944 A.D. by the Arabs and by 1510, the Moors began to settle the region and soon it became a center for the Barbary pirates. Barbarossa seized the city in 1529 and ousted the Spaniards.

The French invasion began in 1830, and a University was founded in 1879. During World War II, Algiers was headquarters for the Allies. The war for independence began in the 1950s and caused considerable damage before Algeria was granted its freedom in 1962.

Constantine

In ancient times, this city was known as Cirta. A new city was built in 313 A.D. by the Roman Emperor Constantine on a rocky plateau surrounded by the Rhumel river. The arab invasion came in 710 A.D. Constantine fell to the French in 1837. A university opened in 1969.

Elevation: 2130 feet

Oran

Oran was founded by Arabs from southern Spain in 903 A.D. It fell to Spanish rule from 1509 until 1708 when the Ottoman Turks took over. A severe earthquake in 1790 did considerable damage. Oran fell to the French in 1831 and it was occupied by the Allies in November 1942 during World War II. A university opened in 1965.

Angola

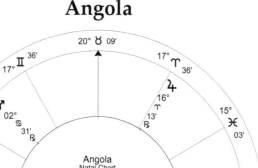

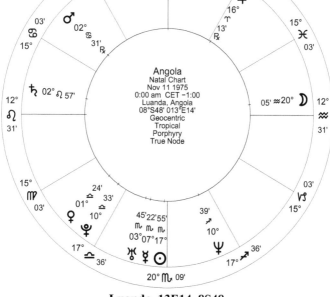

Luanda, 13E14, 8S48
November 11, 1975, 12:00 a.m. MET
Sources: *London Times*, CBS and *San Francisco Chronicle*

The Portuguese began to colonize the region in 1575. Angola became a major source for slaves; more than three million were shipped to Brazil. During the 1950s, the MPLA was founded for liberation from Portugal while the FNLA was founded in the north with the same objective. Another group, UNITA was founded in 1966 in the south.

When independence came in November 1975, a civil war erupted with the aid of the Soviet Union and Cuba. When a peace treaty was signed in May 1991, over more than one million had been killed (progressed ASC sesquare Jupiter, progressed Sun trine Saturn). United Nations peacekeeping forces arrived in February 1994 (progressed ASC sextile Uranus) and left in February 1999, after another 200,000 were killed (progressed Sun conjunct Neptune).

Angola is a country of 12 million people living in an area twice the size of the Ukraine and three times the size of California. From the coast, the land rises to an interior plateau which rises to over 5000 ft. The southern part of the country is part of the Namib desert. The coastline is 994 miles long, including the enclave of Cabinda. The main exports are coffee, oil and diamonds.

Luanda

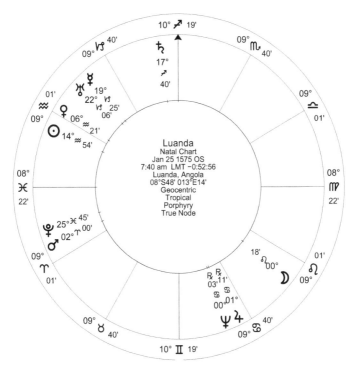

Luanda, 13E14, 8S49
January 25, 1575, 7:40 a.m. LMT
Source: National Library of Portugal

Luanda was founded by Paulo Dias de Bovias as Sao Paulo de Luanda in January 1575 by the Portuguese. It became the capital of Angola in 1627 (progressed MC sextile Mars opposition Moon). The Dutch occupied the region from 1641 to 1648 (progressed MC conjunct Sun sextile Saturn). The slave trade finally ceased in 1888. Oil was discovered in 1955 (progressed MC square Pluto) and a university opened in 1963. Luanda suffered extensively during the Civil War which began in 1975.

Benin

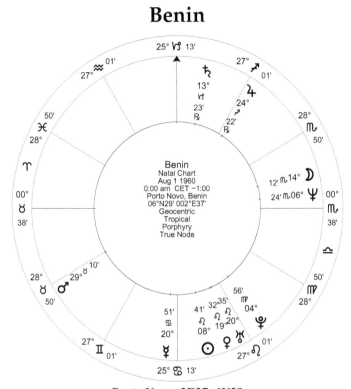

Porto Novo, 2E37, 6N29
August 1, 1960, 12:00 a.m. MET
Sources: *New York Times* and *Los Angeles Times*

The Portuguese arrived in 1485 to this region which became a major supplier for slaves. The Allada Kingdom formed in the south during the 16th century and the following century, the King of Dahomey supported the slave trade which lasted until 1885.

In 1851, a treaty was made with France and by 1893, the French colony of Dahomey was signed sealed and delivered. In 1904, Dahomey became part of French West Africa.

Independence came in August 1960 to Dahomey which was renamed Benin in 1975. Kerekou instituted a military take-over in 1972 (progressed MC square Neptune, progressed ASC trine Saturn, progressed Sun conjunct Uranus). Marxism and socialism were the order of the day until December 1989 when both of them were given the boot (progressed MC sextile Jupiter, progressed ASC conjunct Mars).

Benin is a country of eight million people living in an area the size of Louisiana or Bulgaria. Lagoons line the coastline, which is 75 miles long. Inland comes the flat plains, rain forests and savanna. The chief exports are cotton, palm oil and cocoa.

Cotonou

Cotonou is the chief port and largest city in Benin. During the 19th century it began as a small fishing village. The French began a trading post in 1851, and the region was ceded to France in May 1868. The University of Benin was founded in 1970.

Porto Novo

Porto Novo has been the capital of Benin since 1894 and lies on the Oueme lagoon. During the past centuries, it was a center for the slave trade.

Botswana

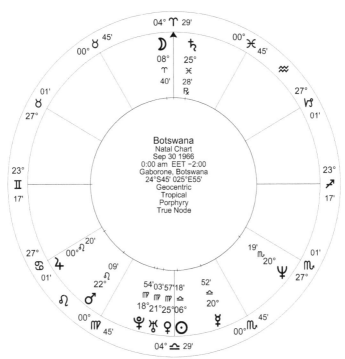

Gaborone, 25E55, 24S45
September 30, 1966, 12:00 a.m. EET
Sources: *London Times*, *New York Times* and *Los Angeles Times*

About 1000 A.D., this was the land of the Tswana, a region of cattle herders. In September 1885, the British established a Protectorate over the region now called Bechuanaland. Its southern part went to South Africa. A new capital was founded at Gaborone in February 1965 and the region attained its independence in late September 1966.

Botswana is a country of more than one and a half million people living in an area the size of Texas or the Ukraine. The southwest contains the Kalahari desert while the remainder is hilly. Over 17 percent of the country is national parks or wildlife reserves. Over one-third of the adults have AIDS. The main exports are copper, diamonds and nickel.

Gaborone

Gaborone became the capital of Botswana in February 1965, after the. government moved from Mafeking. It became home to numerous exiles from South Africa, which is only 12 miles away. The University of Botswana was founded in 1976.

Burkina Faso

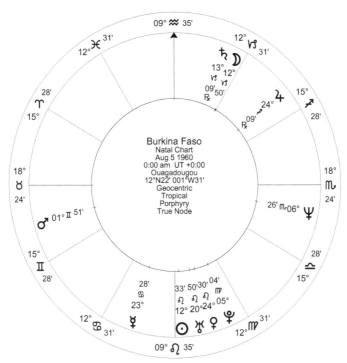

Ouagadougou, 1W31, 12N22
August 5, 1960, 12:00 a.m. GMT
Sources: *New York Times* **and** *Le Monde*

During the 11th century, this region was part of the Mossi King-dom. In 1904, the French made it a colony with Upper Senegal and Niger. In 1919, it became the colony of Upper Volta, a land of three rivers: the Black Volta, the Red Volta and the White Volta.

Independence came from France in August 1960 and the region was renamed Burkina Faso in August 1984. A military coup in 1980 occurred (progressed MC semisquare Saturn, progressed ASC semisquare Mercury, progressed Sun square Mars) and two coups took place in 1989 which were put down (progressed MC sesquare Mercury).

Burkina Faso is a country of 14 million people living in an area the size of Colorado or Italy. This country sits on a plateau from which rivers reach to Ghana or the Niger river. The northern part of the country is part of the Sahel. The main exports are gold, cotton, peanuts and livestock.

Ouagadougou

Ouagadougou was the capital of the Mossi Kingdom during the 15th century. A railroad was completed to Abidjan in 1954 by which time it became the capital of Upper Volta, as the region was then known. A university opened in 1969.

Burundi

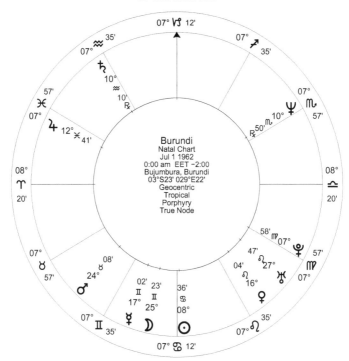

Bujumbura, 29E22, 3S23
July 1, 1962, l2:00 a.m. EET
Sources: *Los Angeles Times* **and** *Le Soir*

During ancient times, this was the land of the Twa (or pygmy) people. The Hutu people arrived around 1000 A.D. and the Tutsi became overlords by the 15th century. Europeans began to explore the region in 1858 and the Germans arrived to take over by 1899.

Belgium took over from the Germans in 1916 during World War I and in May 1920 assumed the mandate over Ruanda-Urundi. Urundi voted to become a monarchy while Ruanda voted to become a republic in 1961. The region became independent of Belgium in July 1962.

Four years later, the Tutsi monarchy ends and a Republic is pro-

13

claimed (progressed MC sextile Jupiter sesquare Uranus, progressed Sun trine Jupiter semisquare Uranus). A rebellion among the Hutu began in 1972 and with the Hutu the following year. Over 150,000 were dead (mostly Hutus) and nearly 100,000 fled the country. A civil war between the two groups erupted in October 1993 after the president and his successor were assassinated (progressed ASC semisquare Moon square Saturn opposition Neptune). More than 250,000 died in the civil war and nearly 350,000 Hutus were living in refugee camps, some in neighboring Zaire. UN troops left in July 1996 (progressed MC sesquare Moon inconjunct Pluto, progressed Sun semisquare Moon opposition Saturn square Neptune).

Burundi is a land of seven million people living in an area the size of Maryland or Albania. It's the second most-densely populated country in Africa. The Great Rift Valley occupies the western region along with Lake Tanganyika, the world's second-deepest lake. In the east are high mountains which descend to plateaus and grassy highlands. The main exports are coffee, tea and cotton.

Bujumbura

Bujumbura, the capital of Burundi, was founded in 1889 by the Germans. In 1960, the University of Bunundi was founded.

Cameroon

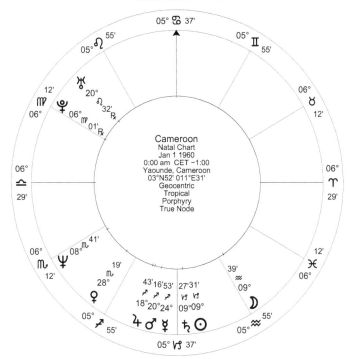

Yaounde, 11E31, 3N52
January 1, 1960, l2: 00 a.m. MET
Source: *New York Times* and *Los Angeles Times*

In ancient times, this was the land of the Bantu people. The Portuguese reached the area in the 1490s and by the 17th century, the southern part of Cameroon became a center for the slave trade. The region became the German Protectoratc of Kamerun in 1884, but during World War I, the region was divided between Britain in the west and France in the east. The French part became independent in January 1960 while the British part voted to join Nigeria.

Cameroon is a land of 17 million people living in an area the size of Sweden. A narrow plain lies along the 250-mile coast which rises to a series of plateaus. Rain forests are found in the

15

south, while a semi-desert occupies the north. Mt. Cameroon, a volcano, lies in the southwest part of the country. The main exports are oil, bauxite, cocoa, coffee, cotton and lumber.

Douala

Douala lies on the Douri river where it meets the Atlantic Ocean. The Portuguese first visited in 1472 but it was left up to the Germans to found the present city in 1884 which they called Kamarunstadt. It was the capital of German Kameroon from 1901 to 1916 and capital of Cameroon from 1940 to 1946.

Yaounde

Yaounde was founded in 1888 by the Germans. The city is overlooked by Mont Febe. In 1926 it became the capital of Cameroon. During World War II the government moved to Douala from 1940 to 1946. The University of Yaounde was founded in 1962.

Cape Verde

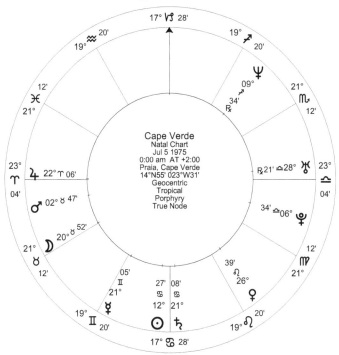

Praia, 23W31, 14N55
July 5, 1975, 12:00 a.m. AZT
Source: *New York Times*

During the 16th century, Cape Verde was a supply station for the slave trade. Three centuries later, whalers were recruited from the USA to aid the local economy. Cape Verde became an overseas province of Portugal in 1951 but five years later, the PAIGC was founded to liberate the islands from Portuguese control altogether.

Cape Verde is a country of 450,000 people living in a region one and a half times the size of Rhode Island or Luxemburg. The islands lie 350 miles west of Dakar in the Atlantic, and all 15 of them are volcanic. The main exports are shoes, fish and bananas.

Central African Republic

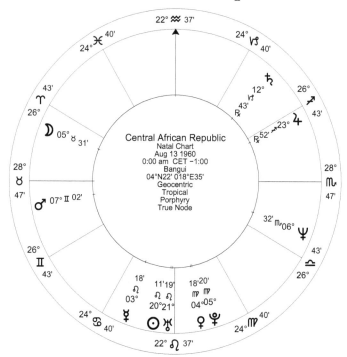

Bangui, 18E35, 4N22
August 13, 1960, 12:00 a.m. MET
Sources: *New York Times* and *Los Angeles Times*

Between the 16th and 19th centuries this region was a slave trade center. The French came in 1889. The territory was first known as Ubangi-Shari after the two major rivers in the region and by 1910 it had become part of French Equatorial Africa. Independence from France came in August 1960.

During the first five years of freedom, the Chinese influence was strong. A rebellion or army coup took place in 1966 in which David Dacko was removed from office and Jean-Bedel Bokassa became the strong man (progressed MC semisquare Saturn, progressed ASC sextile Mercury square Venus and Pluto). Bokassa declared himself Emperor in December 1976 and changed the country's name to the Central African Empire (progressed MC square Mars, progressed ASC inconjunct Saturn, progressed Sun trine Moon sextile Neptune conjunct Pluto). Bokassa was overthrown by his arch-rival David Dacko in September 1979 but two years later, in September 1981, Dacko was ousted in an army coup (progressed MC sextile Saturn).

The Central African Republic is a country of four million people living in a land the size of the Ukraine or Texas. A rolling plateau divides the headwaters of the Ubangi river which flows south from the Shari river which flows north. Rain forests are found in the southwest while savanna predominates in the north. The main exports are diamonds, coffee, cotton, timber and tobacco.

Bangui

Bangui, the capital, was founded in 1899 and named for the Ubangi river. A university was founded here in 1969.

Chad

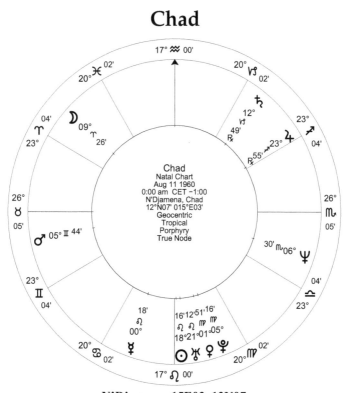

N'Djamena, 15E03, 12N07
August 11, 1960, 12:00 a.m. MET
Sources: *New York Times* and *Los Angeles Times*

This region was part of the vast Kanem-Bornu Empire by 700 A.D. and from the 16th to the 19th century, Arab slave traders plied the area. Chad became a French territory in 1891 and by 1910, it was part of French West Africa. Independence came in August 1960.

A rebellion against religious dominance broke out in 1965 between Moslems in the north and Christians in the south (progressed MC sextile Jupiter opposition Uranus, progressed ASC sextile Mercury, progressed Sun sesquare Moon trine Jupiter). In 1975, Tombalbage was ousted during a coup (progressed MC inconjunct Mercury square Venus, progressed ASC sextile Moon, progressed Sun conjunct Venus).

In December 1980, Libyan support for the rebellion led to their occupation of the northern part of Chad and the beginning of a civil war (progressed MC trine Neptune opposition Pluto, progressed ASC semisquare Mercury). A truce was signed with Libya in May 1988 (progressed MC sesquare Mercury, progressed ASC sextile Uranus, progressed Sun semisquare Mercury).

Chad is a country of 10 million people living in an area twice the size of the Ukraine or three times the area of California. The Sahara occupies the north while in the center is the Sahel and savanna. Forests occupy the southern tier. Lake Chad is the largest body of water. The main exports are cotton and cattle.

N'Djamena

Fort Lamy was founded in late May 1900 by Emile Gentil and named for Amedee-Francois Lamy who had been killed in the battle of Kousseri shortly before. It lies at the junction of the Shari river where it meets the Logone river.

The University of Chad was established in 1971 (progressed MC square Mercury and Jupiter, progressed ASC conjunct Jupiter opposition Mercury). Its name was changed in April 1973 to N'Djamena (progressed MC square Uranus trine Mars progressed ASC Opposition Sun). Beginning in 1979, Chad experienced a major drought which lasted for four years. During this time a civil war broke out which partially destroyed the city (progressed MC square Pluto, progressed ASC conjunct Uranus).

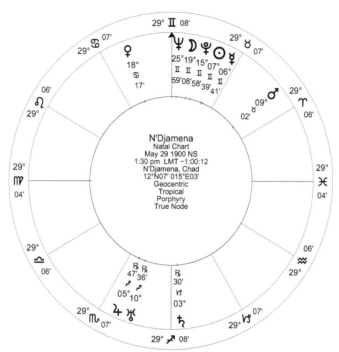

N'Djamena, 15E03, 12N07
May 29, 1900, 11:30 p.m. LMT
Source: Internet

Comoros

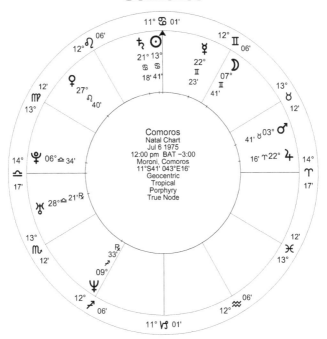

Comoros
Natal Chart
Jul 6 1975
12:00 pm BAT −3:00
Moroni, Comoros
11°S41' 043°E16'
Geocentric
Tropical
Porphyry
True Node

Moroni, 43E16, 11S41
July 6, 1975, 12:00 p.m. BGT
Source: *San Francisco Examiner. Los Angeles Times* and
***International Herald-Tribune* don't give a time of day.**

During the 16th century the Arabs invaded these islands. The French arrived in 1841 but didn't occupy the region until 1909. All island groups voted for independence from France except Mayotte, where freedom came in July 1975. A leftist regime ruled the islands from 1975 to 1978 and the president was assassinated in November 1989 (progressed Sun square Uranus). All in all, more than 20 coups have occurred up to 2005.

The Comoros occupy an area slightly smaller than Rhode Island or Luxembourg. The country consists of three mountainous islands and small coral islands in the Indian Ocean. The coastline is 211 miles long. The chief exports are vanilla and cloves.

Congo

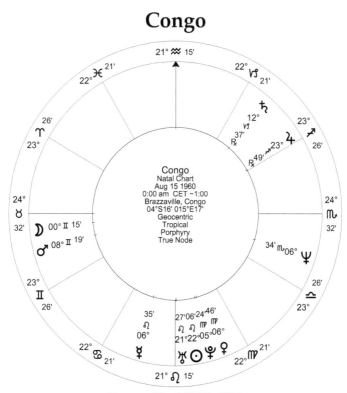

Brazzaville, 15E17, 4S16
August 15, 1960, 12:00 a.m. MET
Source: *Los Angeles Times*

Between the 15th and 18th centuries, this region was part of the Ndonga and Kongo Kingdoms. The French established a protectorate in 1883 and by 1910 it was part of French Equatorial Africa. Independence came in August 1960.

A coup in 1963 instituted Marxism (progressed MC sextile Jupiter, progressed ASC sesquare Saturn) to be followed by another coup in 1968 (progressed MC square Moon progressed ASC conjunct Moon, progressed Sun square Moon). Communism was formally in by 1970 and for the next two decades reigned supreme until 1990 (progressed MC sesquare Mercury and Neptune inconjunct Uranus, progressed ASC semisquare Mercury sesquare Neptune, progressed Sun semisquare Mercury and Neptune).

A rebellion in Brazzaville broke out in 1997 by those loyal to Sassou and by June 2000, an ethnic civil war had erupted (progressed MC sextile Moon, progressed Sun trine Moon).

The Congo is a land of three million people residing in an area the size of Montana or Finland. The country sits on the Equator by the river of the same name. A narrow coastal plain rises to a plateau and savanna in the center. The north is swampy and thickly-forested. The coastline is 105 miles long. The main exports are oil, coffee, cocoa and lumber.

Brazzaville

Brazzaville was founded by Pierre de Brazza in October 1880 on the banks of the Congo river. He named the place after himself; the original town was called Ntomo. In 1910, it became the capital of French Equatorial Africa (progressed MC trine Sun). It was here in 1944 that General de Gaulle decided the post-war future of French overseas colonies. A university was founded in 1972.

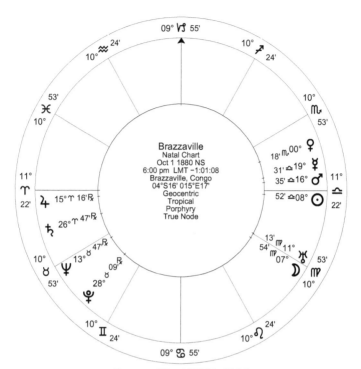

Brazzaville, 15E17, 4S16
October 1, 1880, 6:00 p.m. LMT
Source: National Library of Belgium

Cote D'Ivoire

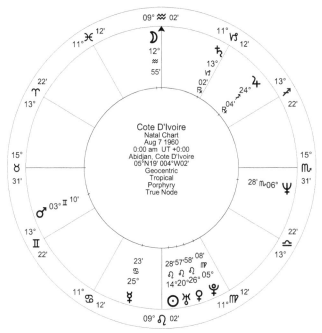

Abidjan, 4W02, 5N19
August 7, 1960, l2:00 a.m. GMT
Source: *Los Angeles Times*

During the 15th century, the Portuguese arrive and the slave trade begins. A French trading post was established in 1637 and in 1842 a French protectorate was established. It became a French colony in 1893 and part of French West Africa in 1904. Independence came in August 1960 with Houphouet-Boigny as its first leader.

In 1983, the capital was planned to move from Abidjan to Yamoussoukro (progressed Sun conjunct Pluto). The country formally changed its name from the Ivory Coast to Cote d'Ivoire in October 1985 (progressed MC square Mars, progressed ASC semisquare Mercury). In February 1990, protests against the long rule of Houphouet-Boigny began (progressed ASC trine Moon,

27

progressed Sun inconjunct Moon trine Saturn). He died in December 1993 (progressed MC sesquare Mercury).

The president was assassinated in a military coup in December 1999 which was led by Gusi (progressed ASC sextile Uranus sesquare Neptune, progressed Sun semisquare Neptune). Gusi was himself assassinated and a civil war began in September 2002 (progressed MC sesquare Neptune, progressed ASC opposition Jupiter, progressed Sun square Jupiter). By the following year, rebels held the north while government troops held the south.

The Cote d'Ivoire, or Ivory Coast, is a country of 17 million people about the size of New Mexico or Norway. Sandbars and lagoons line the coast in the southeast while rocky cliffs tower over the southwestern shore. High plains and the forested Guinea highlands occupy most of the country while savanna dominates the northern tier. The coastline is 320 miles long. Main exports are coffee, cocoa (world's number one) and cotton.

Abidjan

Abidjan is the largest city in the country and the former capital. The Vridi Canal was opened to the Atlantic Ocean and the harbor was expanded. Abidjan was chartered as a Town in 1903.

Yamoussoukro

Yamoussoukro became the capital of the country in 1983. The city is located about 135 miles inland from the coast. The Basilica of Notre Dame de la Paix was completed in 1990 and today is the largest church in Africa.

Djibouti

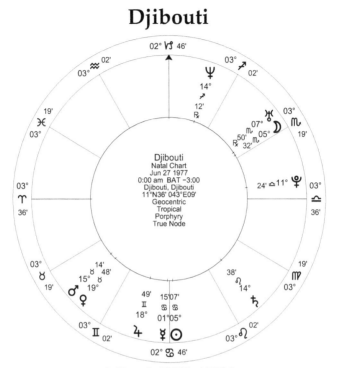

Djibouti, 43E09, 11N36
June 27, 1977, l2:00 a.m. BGT
Sources: *London Times* **and** *San Francisco Chronicle*

Islam arrived in the 9th century and when the French began to occupy the region, a conflict arose in 1862 between the Moslem Afars and the Ethiopian Christians. The Issas (Somalis) moved further south. In 1888, the French established Somaliland and a railroad was built to Addis Ababa. Neighboring Eritrca became part of Ethiopia in 1952. The region was renamed the Territory of Afars and Issas in 1967. Independence came in June 1977.

Ethnic tensions, however, erupted in 1997 in what was called the Afar rebellion (progressed MC trine Mars, progressed Sun sextile Venus) and wasn't settled until three years later in 1994 (progressed MC inconjunct Jupiter).

Djibouti is a country of half a million people who live in an area the size of Vermont or Macedonia. The country has a 195 mile coastline along the Red Sea and the Gulf of Tadjoura. The Mabla Mountains and highlands occupy the northern tier and the south has Lake Assal, the lowest point in Africa some 155 feet below sea level. Over 90 percent of Djibouti is desert. The main exports are hides and animal skins. The chief source of revenue, however, comes from its port and the railroad to Ethiopia.

Djibouti

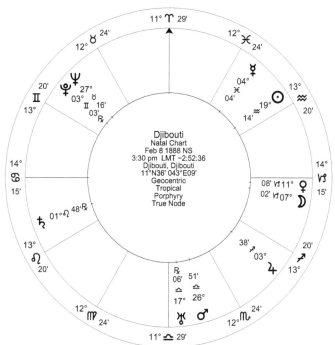

Djibouti, 43E09, 11N36
February 8, 1888, 3:30 p.m. LMT
Source: Archives de France

Djibouti, capital of the country with the same name, lies on the Gulf of Tadjoura, an arm of the Red Sea. It was founded in February 1888 by Leonce Lagarde as a port and was made capital of

French Somaliland in 1896 (progressed MC sextile Sun). A railroad to Addis Ababa was completed in 1917 (progressed ASC opposition Sun) a major lifeline for the land-locked country of Ethiopia.

The British instituted a naval blockade in 1940 to quell Italian forces then occupying Ethiopia (progressed MC conjunct Pluto square Mercury opposition Jupiter). In 1949, Djibouti became a free port, but suffered considerably from 1967 to 1975 when Egypt closed the Suez Canal (progressed ASC sextile Saturn).

Egypt

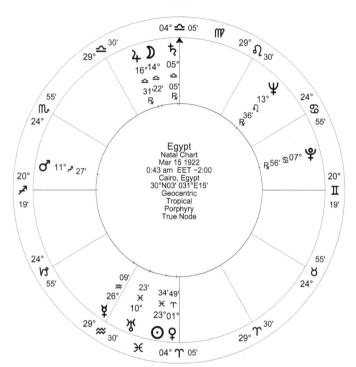

Cairo, 31E15, 30N03
March 15, 1922, 12:43 a.m. EET
Sources: *Egyptian Gazette* and *London Times*

Egyptian Republic

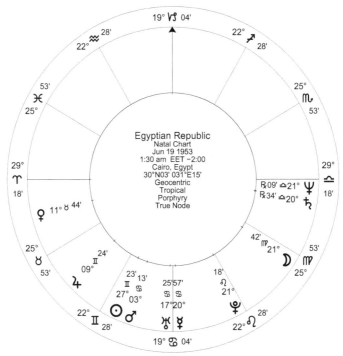

Cairo, 31E15, 30N03
June 19, 1953, 1:30 a.m. EET
Source: BBC

Egyptian civilization began about 5000 B.C.; by around 3200 B.C., a Unified Kingdom of Upper and Lower Egypt existed from Nubia in the south to Syria in the northeast. This was the time of pyramid-building and the time when the exotic and fascinating cities of Luxor, Memphis and Thebes were constructed. The Temple of Karnak and Abu-Simbel were built. The most famous ruler of this time of many dynasties was Rameses II who lived around the time that the Israelites were freed and their Exodus which took them over the Red (or Reed) Sea on their way back to the promised land.

The Persians invaded Egypt in 341 B.C., a full decade before Greek occupation took place with the founding of the city of Alexandria in 331 B.C. Roman occupation began in 30 B.C. when Cleopatra and her lover, Marc Antony, passed into the great beyond. The Byzantines took over from the Romans between the 3rd and 7th centuries A.D. when the Arabs arrived in 639 A.D. The Ottomans came in 1567 and stayed until the 19th century.

The French were originally contracted to build the Suez Canal in 1859. Ten years later in November 1869 the canal was opened to shipping. It cut the journey to the Orient by over 6000 miles which was very important to the British whose "jewel in the Crown" were the riches of India. The British occupation of Egypt began in 1882, seven years after they had assumed administration of the Suez Canal. In December 1914, the British assumed a Protectorate over Egypt during the early days of World War I.

Partial independence was granted in March 1922 and the Battle of El Alamein took place in 1942 when the Allies triumphed and the Axis was defeated (progressed MC inconjunct Sun, progressed ASC opposition Pluto, progressed Sun opposition Moon) In July 1952, King Farouk was ousted in a coup by Gamal Abdel Nasser (progressed ASC square Jupiter). Israel's independence in May 1948 brought all Arab armies to that region (progressed ASC inconjunct Neptune) to destroy the newly-born nation whose military strength surprised everyone.

In July 1956, the Suez Canal was nationalized (progressed MC sextile Mars) which prompted a war with Israel by October 1956. In February 1958, Egypt joined with Syria and Yemen to form the United Arab Republic (progressed MC sesquare Jupiter) but it fell apart in 1961 (progressed MC inconjunct Sun progressed ASC conjunct Venus, progressed Sun semisquare Pluto). Another war with Israel erupted in June 1967 (progressed MC inconjunct Mars, progressed ASC sextile Urmnus, progressed Sun sextile Venus). The Suez Canal was closed in 1970, the same year General Nasser died (progressed ASC trine Moon inconjunct Neptune square Pluto).

The fourth and final war with Israel erupted in October 1973 (progressed MC trine Jupiter, progressed Sun conjunct Uranus). This eventually led to a signing of a peace treaty in March 1979 whereby Egypt regained control of the Sinai (progressed MC sesquare Sun, progressed Sun sextile Moon conjunct Mercury). Because many of those in the Egyptian military thought President Sadat a traitor, he was assassinated in October 1981 during a military review (progressed MC inconjunct Uranus, progressed ASC semisquare Uranus, progressed Sun semisquare Jupiter).

Egypt is a land of 80 million people, the second most-populous nation in Africa. It occupies an area about twice the size of Spain or one and a half times the size of Texas. Most of Egypt is part of the Sahara and most of the people live along the Nile River, the longest body of water in the world. The highest point lies in the Sinai peninsula, Gebel Katherina (elev. 8650 ft.) and the lowest point is the Qattara Depression which lies 133 ft. below sea level. The coastline is 1523 miles long fronting the Mediterranean and Red Seas. Technically and geographically, the Sinai peninsula is part of Asia. Egypt is the second-largest industrial power in Africa and the main exports are crude oil, cotton and textiles.

Cairo

Cairo was originally founded as a military camp on November 8, 641 A.D. on the banks of the Nile river. The present city was founded in August 969 A.D. and called Al Qahira or "Mars the victorious" as Mars was rising just above the ASC. It became the capital of Egypt in 973 A.D. (progressed MC square Jupiter, progressed ASC sextile Mercury) one year after Al-Azhar University was founded, the largest in the Arab world.

Al Fustat was burned by the Crusaders in 1168 (progressed ASC opposition Mars/Jupiter) and Cairo became capital of the Mameluke Empire in 1260 (progressed ASC trine Sun opposition Neptune).

In 1303, a massive earthquake caused extensive damage (progressed MC opposition Pluto sextile Jupiter, progressed ASC sesquare Uranus) and the Black Death (plague) killed thousands (progressed ASC square Neptune) in this city of over 500,000 peo-

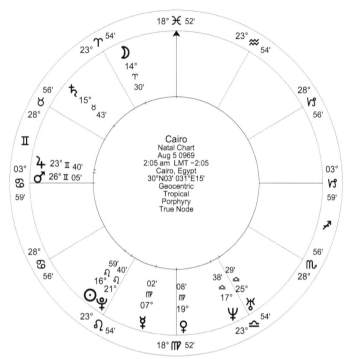

Cairo, 31E15, 30N03
August 5, 969 AD, 2:00 a.m. LMT
Source: *National Geographic*

ple. Tamerlane attacked Cairo in 1400 (progressed ASC sextile Mars, Jupiter and Uranus). With Da Gama's discovery of a route around Africa in 1498, Cairo's fortunes began to wane. The Ottoman occupation began in 1517 leading to over three centuries of neglect (progressed ASC trine Moon).

Napoleon arrived in 1798 and for a moment conquered Egypt. The Turks recaptured the country three years later (progressed MC semisquare Sun). Another strong earthquake hit the city in 1847 (progressed MC conjunct Sun, progressed ASC sesquare Moon). The city was rebuilt along Parisian lines beginning in 1863 (progressed MC sesquare Moon).

Cairo began the 20th century with more than 600,000 inhabitants; five decades later it had more than two million residents. The War with Israel in June 1967 put Cairo in harms way (progressed MC trine Sun, progressed ASC semisquare Uranus). The subway was opened in 1987 (progressed MC trine Mercury). Another very strong earthquake struck the city in 1992 (progressed ASC trine Sun opposition Neptune).

East of the Nile river sits Old Cairo, a walled enclave which houses more than 500 mosques. The Citadel, built by Saladin in 1176, divides Old Cairo from New Cairo. One of the most popular sights in Cairo is the Egyptian Museum where King Tut has his own exhibition. West of the Nile is El Giza, home to the Pyramids and the Sphinx. The ancient city of Memphis lies 25 miles south as does the old city of Saqqara, home of the Zoser step pyramid.

Alexandria

Alexandria lies on the shores of the Mediterranean Sea some 115 miles northwest of Cairo. The city was founded by Alexander the Great and it became the capital in 330 B.C. (ASC square Sun). The Pharos Lighthouse was begun in 280 B.C. (progressed MC trine Jupiter) and the world-famous Library at Alexandria. Begun in the 3rd century B.C., it housed more than 500,000 volumes, one for each of its inhabitants. The Romans arrived in 80 B.C. (progressed ASC square Venus) and the last Greek ruler, Queen Cleopatra committed suicide in 30 B.C. (progressed MC square Neptune and Pluto trine Venus, progressed ASC square Mars). Rome then took over Egypt.

St. Mark made his first convert to Christianity in 45 A.D. (progressed MC conjunct Sun, progressed ASC opposition Jupiter). By 330 A.D., the city was ruled from Constantinople as its occupation by the Byzantine Empire began. In 391 A.D., the famed Library was burned by Theodosius and over 700,000 volumes were lost (progressed ASC conjunct Uranus). The Persians ousted the Byzantines in 616 and the Arabs came in 642 (progressed MC opposition Venus). Over the next few centuries, the Nile delta silted up and Alexandria lost much of its importance.

The Ottomans conquered the region in 1517 (progressed MC

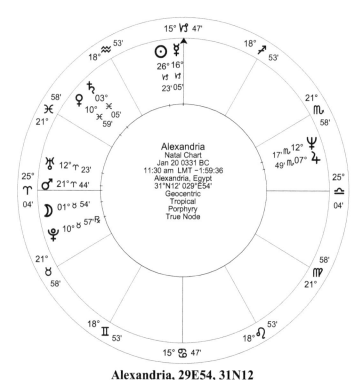

Alexandria, 29E54, 31N12
January 20, 331 BC, at 11:30 a.m.
Source: *Chronicle of African History* by G. Freeman-Grenville

square Jupiter). By the time Napoleon arrived in 1798, Alexandria had only 6000 people. Three years later, the British took over (progressed ASC opposition Sun) and the Mahmudiya Canal opened in 1818 thus unblocking the harbor (progressed MC square Saturn). In 1852, the first railroad in Africa was completed to Cairo (progressed MC sextile Jupiter) and in November 1869, the Suez Canal opened and Alexandria's fortunes increased considerably (progressed ASC conjunct Uranus opposition Jupiter). The British bombarded the city in 1882 (progressed MC square Jupiter).

Today, Alexandria handles 75 percent of Egypt's imports and exports. It's also a tourist destination with more than nine miles of beaches fronting the Mediterranean.

Alexandria was an Allied naval base during World War I (progressed MC conjunct Venus) and the Germans bombarded the city in 1942 during World War II (progressed MC inconjunct Jupiter). In 2000 the new Bibliotheca Alexandria was completed.

The ancient library was also a research institute and university, astronomical observatory and chemical laboratory. It also had botanical and zoological gardens and a 500-bed hospital. Over 14,000 students attended these facilities and were taught mathematics, science, literature, philosophy and medicine.

Incorporated: 1895

The Great Pyramid

Probably no other structure in the world evokes as much interest or mystery as does the Great Pyramid of Egypt. It is variously called the Pyramid of Cheops or Khufu as well. It is located at latitude 29N59 and longitude 31E09, a few miles southwest of the present city of Cairo. It sits at an elevation of 198 feet above sea level. The Pyramid complex consists of nine pyramids including the monuments dedicated to Chephren and Mycerinus. These are not the oldest pyramids in Egypt—the step pyramid of Zoser was erected around 2700 B.C. This pyramid complex appears to have been constructed shortly afterwards.

The Pyramid was never intended to be the tomb of a Pharaoh. It appears to be a monument in stone which has recorded various astronomical, mathematical and geological information in stone. Some 2.5 million blocks were used in the construction; most of the stones weighed 2.5 tons. How they were placed at such a great height and where the stone came from is a mystery for the ages. Many theories have been put forth as to how the Pyramid was constructed, but we may never know the whole truth. The 2.5-ton blocks of stone appear to have come from a quarry further up the Nile and floated down the Nile on barges. If a causeway was built to place these blocks one upon the other, it would have taken longer than the accepted 20 years to build it unless the Egyptians had outside help.

There is something really strange about the fact that salt water occupies the outside of the Pyramid up to about 225 feet. The monument could have been constructed before the Great Flood mentioned in the Bible a a precaution for mankind retaining the secrets of the universe. Nobody knows exactly when the flood occurred, only that about half of the Pyramid was at one time under water. The usually accepted date of construction is placed somewhere during the 27th century B.C. If, as I believe, the Sphinx was built around the time that the Great Age moved from Virgo to Leo, then the Pyramid was built even before that. That would place its construction more than 12,000 years ago. The Sphinx is the body of a lion with the head of a woman. What better description for the transformation from one Great Age to another?

The height of the Great Pyramid is measured in Pyramid inches, which equates to 1.00106 British and American inches. The height of this enigmatic monument is 5,813 inches, which is shown by measuring from the base to the top of the original capstone. The Pyramid was once faced with gleaming limestone that could probably have been seen as a beacon from outer space. The limestone was carted away during the 13th century, after a massive earthquake, to construct new buildings and structures in the neighboring city of Cairo.

The 5,813-inch height of this structure is also shown by the distance from the front entrance through to the farthest extremity of the interior passages and chambers. The length of the sides is 755.75 feet, and the entire structure covers 13 acres. The sides were oriented to the cardinal points to within fewer than three inches off true north. If you were to drawn lines from the Pyramid to each point of the compass, you would find that exactly 25 percent of the world's landmass lies in each quadrant. When you draw two angles of 45 degrees northward, the entire delta of the Nile River is thereby enclosed.

With the astronomical, geologic and chronological accuracy needed to construct the Pyramid, the only people who could have done it may have been the Atlanteans, which argues for extra-terrestrials lifting the stones (possibly by levitation) using their superior machines. Was it a navigation marker? It was definitely not a tomb. Or was it a religious temple? We'll probably never know for sure. There were no daily reports from CNN or the Internet in those days and ancient records from Greek travelers are sketchy at best.

From ancient writings we do know that it was used as a religious temple. Initiates first entered the edifice through the wall into the Chamber of Chaos, then up the Descending Passages into the Ascending Passage at the end of which was the Queens Chamber. Then the initiates went back through the Grand Gallery, over the Great Step and into the Kings Chamber. It's ironic that the Ascending Passage rises at the same angle as does the Descending Passage. Also, the temperature inside the Great Pyramid remains the same throughout the year despite the torrid heat of summer and the cold blasts of winter. It was clearly erected for a spiritual purpose, among other things, and was intended to serve as a marker for all time. When Napoleon tried to conquer Egypt in the late 18th century, he spent a night inside the Great Pyramid and was said to have had a vision of his destiny. He never spoke of his encounter, but his face illustrated a secret and arcane message. The same has occurred to others who have spent considerable time inside.

As a mathematical storehouse, the Pyramid holds some striking clues regarding Earth's relationship to the universe. The four sides are 9,131 inches long; multiply this by four and it equals 36,524, the length of the Solar Year. The height of the Pyramid is 5,813 inches, which, when multipliled by one million equals 147,804,000. Taken as kilometers rather than miles, this equals the distance of Earth from the Sun. This is also shown in half the diagonal of the base of the Pyramid. The ratio between the diagonal and height is 9:10. The height of the Pyramid used as a radius makes a circle whose area equals that of its base; hence, the structure is perfectly proportioned.

Using the length of the King's Chamber as diameter, a circle also equals the area (in sacred cubits) to the base of the Pyramid. A pyramid inch equals .0254264 meters; the sacred cubit equals 25 pyramid inches or .63566 meters. Multiply this figure by 10 million and the result is 6,356,600 meters, which equates to the polar radius.

The precession of the equinoxes is shown in the diagonals of the Pyramid; 12,913.3 inches multiplied by two equals 25,826.6 years. Pretty close. The precession is also shown in the distance from the ceiling of the Kings Chamber to the cusp (top), which is 4,110.5 inches. This equals the radius of procession. Some say the precession takes 25,920 years and curiously this equals the number of breaths we take each day, and our average pulse rate of 72 beats per minute equals the average lifespan today. There is definitely a human and cosmic correlation. Maybe this is what the Pyramid is trying to tell us.

100 million Pyramid inches equals 2,572,640. Taken again as kilometers, this equates to the speed of Earth's daily rotation. The difference of 1,117 kilometers is attributed to the present daily speed which is 2,571,523 kilometes per day.

Pi is shown by the sum of the sides of the Pyramid (9,131 inches times 4) divided by twice the height (5,813 nches times 2), which equals 3.14157. Spatial Pi (3.2020) is shown by the height of the Pyramid minus the capstone, which is 5,703 inches. The total weight of the Great Pyramid is 5,955,000 tons. Multiply this by one trillin and the result is the weight of Earth. The volume of the Pyramid is 90 million cubic feet.

The difference between the perimeter of the solid base and the base after the addition of casing stones is 286.1022 inches, called the displacement factor. This is also shown in the Grand Gallery, which is 286.1 inches higher than the Ascending Passage. Half way along the side of the Pyramid there is a depression 35.76 inches deep. Multiply this by 8 and the result is 286.08 inches. The first four digits of this figure (286.1) equals the number 17, which coincidentally equals the number of steps to the entrance of the Great Pyramid.

Some scientists and archaeologists have found a strange correlation between Pyramid inches and the course of history during the past 4,000 years. According to this theory, Abraham arrived at the

Promised Land in 2083 B.C.; Moses led the Israelites in their Exodus out of Egypt on April 4, 1486 B.C.; Jesus the Christ of Nazareth was born October 4, 4 B.C., began his ministry October 3, 27 A.D. and was crucified in Jerusalem April 7, 30 A.D. Ironically, the Grand Gallery contains the history of the Jewish people from 30 A.D. until 1909 A.D. All historical measurements stop at September 17, 2001 A.D. The datum line supposedly begins at 2141 B.C. and accordingly the Pyramid was built in 2623 B.C. There are 1,485 years between the Exodus and the Crucifixion. According to this time line, the Exodus took place in 1453 B.C.; add 1,485 years and the result is the 33 A.D. for the Crucifixion. Both charts are included here.

Further investigation yields the birthdate of Jesus the Christ to be September 29, 2 B.C. (1 Tishri), his Baptism on October 14, 29 A.D. and his death on April 3, 33 A.D. The Christ triangle equals 33 years, six months and five days according to the Hebrew calendar, the length of Christ's life on Earth.

The end of the chronology in the Grand Gallery equates to the year 1914. Daniel's prophecy in the Bible equates to 360 (one year) times 7, which equals 2,520. Taken from the fall of Assyria in 607 B.C., adding 2,520 years equals 1914. The chronology also states that World War I would last 52 months, which it did.

Getting back to the astronomical and mathematical information, the coffin inside the Pyramid (but seemingly never used for a dead body) is descriptive of various weights and measures. For example, the U.S. silver dollar contains 412.5 grains, the length of the Kings Chamber. The half dollar (206.2 grains) and quarter dollar (103.1 grains) show this as well. For mathematicians, the angle of the Great Pyramid is 51 degrees 51 seconds 14.3 minutes, close to the septile aspect.

The distance to the Sun from Earth is about 92 million miles. From the four corner sockets to the apex of the Pyramid, the sides slope inward about 10 feet for every nine feet of elevation. Multiplying the height of the Pyramid times 10 for nine times gives the figure of 91,856,060, the distance from Earth to Sun. The average height of Earth above sea level is 455 feet; the height of the Pyra-

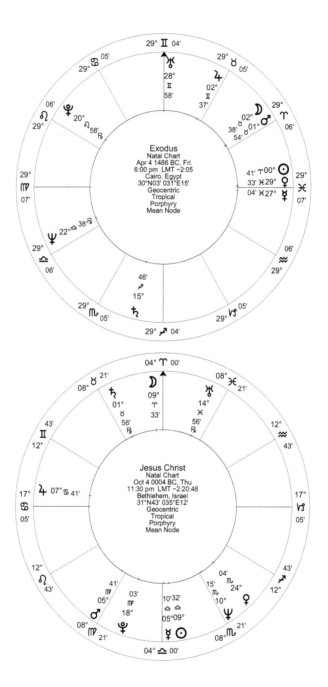

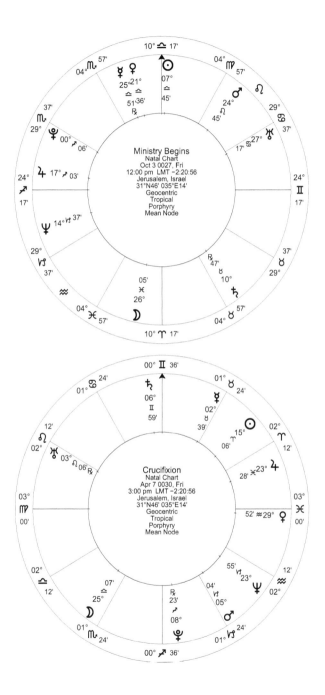

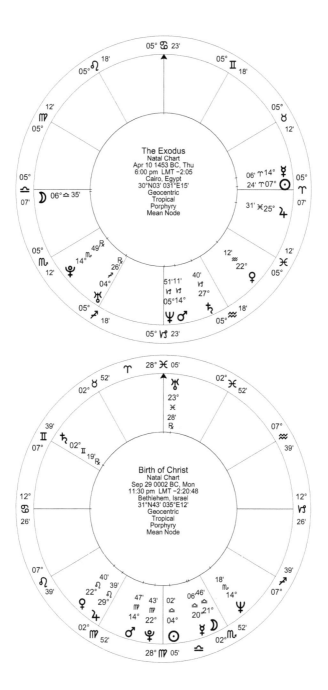

The Exodus
Natal Chart
Apr 10 1453 BC, Thu
6:00 pm LMT −2:05
Cairo, Egypt
30°N03' 031°E15'
Geocentric
Tropical
Porphyry
Mean Node

Birth of Christ
Natal Chart
Sep 29 0002 BC, Mon
11:30 pm LMT −2:20:48
Bethlehem, Israel
31°N43' 035°E12'
Geocentric
Tropical
Porphyry
Mean Node

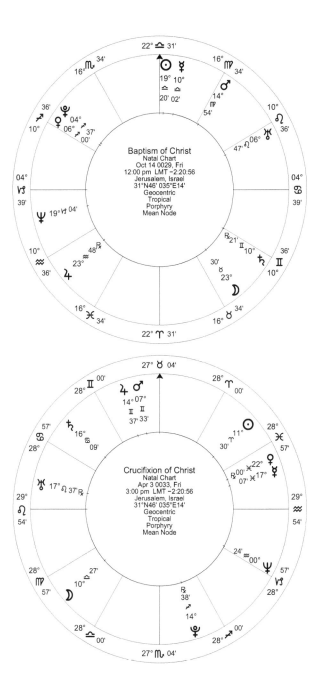

Baptism of Christ
Natal Chart
Oct 14 0029, Fri
12:00 pm LMT −2:20:56
Jerusalem, Israel
31°N46' 035°E14'
Geocentric
Tropical
Porphyry
Mean Node

Crucifixion of Christ
Natal Chart
Apr 3 0033, Fri
3:00 pm LMT −2:20:56
Jerusalem, Israel
31°N46' 035°E14'
Geocentric
Tropical
Porphyry
Mean Node

mid is 454.5 feet. The mean temperature of Earth is 68 degrees, about one-fifth of the distance between the freezing and boiling ponts of water at Fahrenheit. This is the year-round temperature inside the Pyramid.

I'm sure that the foregoing has piqued your interest. There are a number of books and Internet articles that relate to the only surviving Wonder of th Ancient World. Good luck with your research.

Equatorial Guinea

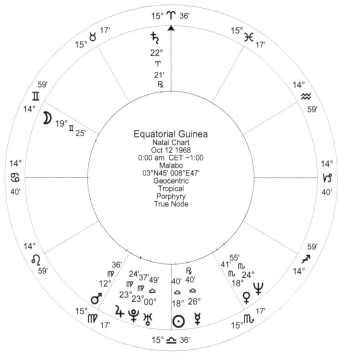

Malabo, 8E47, 3N45
October 12, 1968, 12:00 a.m. MET
Source: *Los Angeles Times*

The Portuguese arrived on Bioto island in 1473 and remained for two centuries until the island was ceded to Spain in 1778. Four years later, yellow fever struck and the Spanish left. It became a province of Spain in 1959. Independence came in October 1968.

A war between the two main regions, Fernando Po and Rio Muni on the mainland, erupted the following year. Foreign workers were expelled in 1976 (progressed MC conjunct Saturn inconjunct Jupiter Neptune and Pluto, progressed ASC square Saturn, progressed Sun conjunct Mercury semisquare Mars). In August 1979, the tyrant, Macias Nguema, was overthrown at long last

49

(progressed MC opposition Mercury sesquare Mars, progressed ASC sextile Jupiter and Pluto trine Neptune). During his infamous reign, over one-third of the population was reputedly killed or exiled.

Equatorial Guinea is a country of half a million people living in an area the size of Maryland or Albania. The mainland is called Rio Muni which has a narrow coastal plain which rises to a high plateau. Bioko Island (formerly Fernando Poo) and five other islands lie off the west African coast, the highest point being Pico de Basile (elev. 9868 ft.) which is a volcano. The main exports are oil, cocoa and timber.

Malabo

Malabo, the capital, was discovered by the Portuguese in 1472 and two years later, the first settlement was made on the rim of a volcanic crater. The Spanish occupied the region in 1778. Malabo is an oil town with several refineries and oil derricks in the harbor.

Eritrea

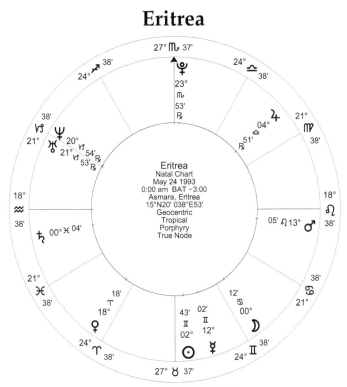

Asmara, 38E53, 15N20
May 24, 1993, 12:00 a.m. BGT
Source: *The Independent*

In ancient times, this region was part of the Kingdom of Axum. Eritrea became an Italian colony in 1890 and remained so until 1941 when the British captured the area. It was part of the Ethiopian federation from 1952 until May 1993 when it attained independence.

A border war with Ethiopia broke out in May 1998 (progressed MC opposition Sun sesquare Venus, progressed ASC opposition Pluto) and lasted until June 2000 (progressed MC sextile Jupiter semisquare Neptune, progressed Sun sesquare Uranus).

Eritrea is a country of five million people living in an area the size of Pennsylvania or Greece. Low Coastal plains dominate the south, while the north is quite mountainous. The coastline along the Red Sea is 680 miles long. The main exports are livestock and sorghum. Asmara is the capital and largest city in the country.

Ethiopia

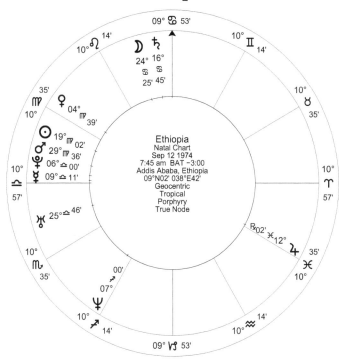

Addis Ababa, 38E42, 9N02
September 12, 1974 7:45 a.m. BGT
Sources: *San Francisco Chronicle* and the Embassy of Ethiopia

During ancient times, a monarchy reportedly traced to the Queen of Sheba and her son, Menelik whose father was probably King Solomon of Israel established a line that reigned for nearly 3000 years. About 330 A.D., Christians (Coptics) began to occupy the highlands while the Moslems who arrived in the 7th century occupied the lowlands. Portuguese explorers visited the region as traders in 1493.

The Emperor Haile Selassie began his rule in 1930, shortly before the Italians invaded his country in 1936. The British defeated Italy in 1941 during World War II. Eritrea joined Ethiopia in 1952 and a revolt with that region erupted in 1961.

Haile Selassie was deposed in September 1974 and the monarchy abolished. The Somalis invaded the Ogaden region in 1977 (progressed MC trine Jupiter). During the 1980s, Ethiopia was beset by a civil war and famine as the Marxist ideology of the country came into question. By 1984, over 1 million had died in the famine (progressed MC sextile Sun semisquare Venus, progressed ASC semisquare Neptune, progressed Sun opposition Mars). In February 1991, the Marxist military regime collapsed thanks to six rebel armies (progressed MC sesquare Jupiter square Uranus, progressed ASC sesquare Jupiter, progressed Sun conjunct Pluto).

In May 1998 a border war with Eritrea broke out (progressed ASC semisquare Sun, progressed Sun inconjunct Jupiter). The war ended in June 2000 (progressed MC sextile Pluto).

Ethiopia is a land of 75 million people living in an area the size of France and the Ukraine combined or three times the area of Montana. Its population is almost equally-divided between Christian and Moslem. Ethiopia is a rugged and mountainous country sitting on a plateau which rises from 6000 to 10,000 feet in elevation. The Great Rift Valley is the defining geographical characteristic. In the north is Ras Dashen (elev. 15,157 ft.) and Lake Tana, the source of the Blue Nile. Grasslands dot the north while savanna rules the south. The main exports are coffee, hides, skins and gold.

Addis Ababa

Addis Ababa is the capital, founded in 1887 by Emperor Taitu and became the headquarters for government in 1896, the same year the Coptic Cathedral was begun. The Univ. of Addis Ababa was founded in 1950. Elevation of Addis Ababa is 8000 feet.

Gabon

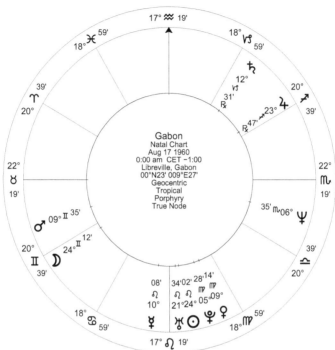

Libreville, 9E27, 0N23
August 17, 1960, l2:00 a.m. MET
Source: *New York Times* and *Los Angeles Times*

Portuguese explorers visited the region in the 1470s looking for slaves. The British, French and Dutch arrived in the 16th century for the same reason. The French began to settle Gabon in 1839. By the 1880s, Gabon became a French colony. It was made part of French West Africa in 1910. Three years later, Dr. Albert Schweitzer arrived from Europe and founded a hospital at Lambarene which today is one of the finest hospitals in Africa.

Independence came in August 1960. The French quelled an attempted coup in 1964 (progressed MC opposition Uranus, progressed ASC sesquare Saturn, progressed Sun square Saturn/Pluto sesquare Saturn). Today, Gabon is one of the most stable nations on the continent.

Gabon is a country of only 1.5 million people in an area the size of Colorado or the United Kingdom. Over 75 percent of the country is rain forest. The savanna covers the east and south and a narrow coastal plain with lagoons rise to interior plateaus. The coastline is 550 miles long.

The main exports are oil and gas, manganese (world's number one), timber and uranium.

Libreville

Libreville, the capital, was founded on the north shore of the Gabon river during the 16th century by the Mpongwe people. The present city was founded in 1843 as a settlement for freed slaves, hence its name. Originally, it was called Fort d'Aumale and was capital of French Equatorial Africa from 1888 until 1904. Omar Bongo University was founded in 1970.

Gambia

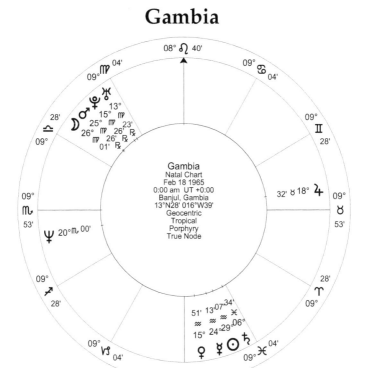

Banjul, l6W39, 13N28
February 18, 1965, l2:00 a.m. GMT
Sources: *London Times, New York Times* and *Los Angeles Times*

Portuguese sailors reached this part of the Mali Empire in 1455. By 1588, the British buy trade rights as the slave trade increased. Gambia also became Britain's first African colony at this time. The British, however, didn't begin to settle the region until 1662.

In 1783, the French ceded the region which was to become Senegambia and in April 1816, the city of Bathurst was founded to quell the slave trade. Gambia became a British colony in December 1888 and achieved independence in February 1965.

In 1981, an attempted coup was defeated by Senegal, the same year the Confederation of Senegambia was formed (progressed

MC opposition Mercury, progressed ASC square Mercury, progressed Sun opposition Pluto). The confederation lasted for eight years. President Jawara was deposed in a coup by Jammeh in July 1994 (progressed ASC square Saturn).

Gambia is a land of 1.5 million people living in a area of only 4500 square miles, the smallest country on mainland Africa. It's only 30 miles across and about 295 miles long. The country sits astride the River Gambia, completely surrounded by Senegal. The 50 mile long coastline has mangrove swamps and the highest point is only 118 feet high. The main exports are peanuts, fish and cotton.

Banjul

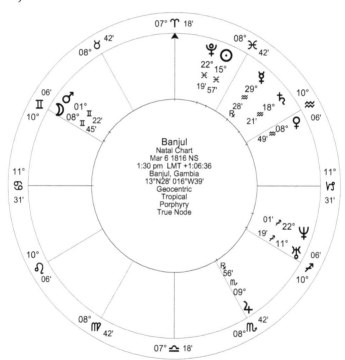

Banjul, 16W39, 13N28
March 6, 1816, 1:30 p.m. LMT
Source: City Hall

Banjul was founded in March 1816 by Capt. Grant to suppress the slave trade. Its original name was Bathurst; it became Banjul in 1973 (progressed ASC opposition Moon). It became the capital of Gambia in 1889 (progressed MC square Pluto). The place was re-built during the 1930s after floods almost wiped the town off the map.

Incorporated: 1946 (town), 1965 (city)

Ghana

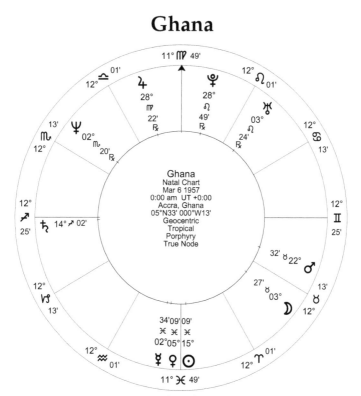

Accra, 0W13, 5N33
March 6, 1957, 12:00 a.m. GMT
Source: *London Times* and *New York Times*

From about 400 A.D. until 1240, this region was part of the Ghana Empire along the Niger river. In 1471, the Portuguese arrived on what was to become the Gold Coast and in the 17th century, it was a center for the slave trade. Dutch, Swedish and British posts lined its shores. In 1807, the slave trade ended and the British took over the region. Ghana became a British Protectorate in 1871 and the British colony in 1886.

Independence came in March 1957, the first British colony to be granted freedom. Its first leader was Kwame Nkrumah who unfortunately looked to the East Germans and Chinese for assistance.

He was deposed in February 1966 along with his Communist cronies. Coups occurred in 1972 (progressed MC opposition Jupiter) 1978 (progressed MC inconjunct Moon and Mercury sextile Uranus) and 1981 which brought Rawlings to power (progressed MC inconjunct Venus sesquare Mars, progressed ASC trine Moon).

Ghana is a country of 22 million people living in an area the size of Oregon or Romania. The 335 mile coastline has many lagoons while the interior southwest is a rainforest on a plateau. The north is dominated by savanna. Ghana has Lake Volta and the Black and White Volta rivers which empty into the Gulf of Guinea. The main exports are cocoa, timber and gold.

Accra

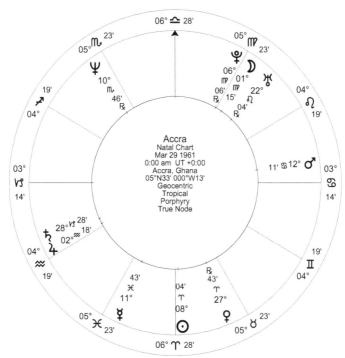

Accra, 0W13, 5N33
March 29, 1961, 12:00 a.m.
Source: Library Board

The Portuguese arrived in 1481 and took Elmina and built St. George castle. The region was settled two years later. Between 1650 and 1680 the British, Dutch and Danes established trading posts. The Dutch were ousted in 1850 and the Danes left in 1872. The Swedes built Chateau Christiansborg in 1662.

In 1877, Accra became capital of the Gold Coast and in 1948, the Univ. of Ghana was founded. The earthquakes of 1862 and 1939 caused extensive damage.

Incorporated: March 1961 (city), 1898 (town)

Guinea

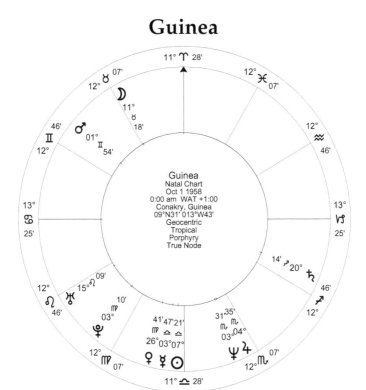

Conakry, 13W43, 9N31
October 1, 1958, 12:00 a.m. WAT
Sources: *New York Times* **and** *Los Angeles Times*

From about 1240 until the beginning of the 16th century, this region was part of the Mali Empire which was succeeded by the Songhai Empire. During the mid-15th century, the Portuguese arrived and the slave trade began. The French came in 1895 and made it a colony. Guinea became part of French West Africa in 1910.

Independence came in October 1958. The first leader, Sekou Toure turned to the USSR and China for support. His reign came to an end in April 1984 with his death (progressed ASC square Jupiter sesquare Saturn, progressed Sun conjunct Neptune sextile

Pluto). A refugee crisis erupted in 2001 when the countries of Liberia and Sierra Leone erupted into civil war (progressed ASC semisquare Sun, progressed Sun semisquare Sun/Mercury).

Guinea contains 10 million people living in an area the size of Oregon or the United Kingdom. The 199 mile coastline is swampy. In the northwest are the Upper Niger plains and savanna, the source of the Senegal, Niger and Gambia rivers. The southeast is forested and a plateau occupies the north. The main exports are diamonds and coffee. Guinea exports 25 percent of the world's bauxite, the world's second-largest producer.

Conakry

Conakry, the capital, was founded in 1884 by the French. Nine years later, it became capital of the colony. A university was founded in 1962.

Guinea Bissau

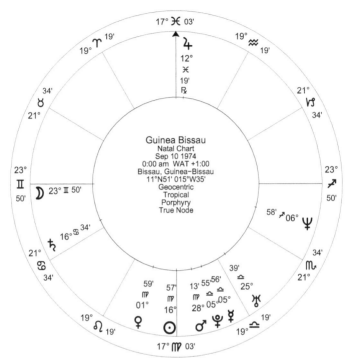

Guinea Bissau
Natal Chart
Sep 10 1974
0:00 am WAT +1:00
Bissau, Guinea–Bissau
11°N51' 015°W35'
Geocentric
Tropical
Porphyry
True Node

Bissau, 15W35, 11N51
September 10, 1974, 12:00 a.m. WAT
Source: *London Times* and *The Guardian*

In ancient times, this area was part of the Ghana and Mali Empires. The Portuguese came in 1446 and the slave trade in the 17th and 18th century filled the coffers in Lisbon. The colony of Portuguese Guinea was created in 1879. The movement for independence began in 1956 and a guerrilla war erupted in 1961. Independence was granted in September 1974 despite the fact that Portuguese Guinea wanted to join Cape Verde.

An army coup took place in November 1980 and the dictator Vieira was brought to power (progressed MC square Moon, progressed ASC square Mars, progressed Sun square Moon). The

65

civil war broke out with an uprising within the army in June 1998 but the country returned to civilian rule in January 2000.

Guinea Bissau is a country 1.5 million people living in an area the size of Belgium. The 217 mile coastline is a low-lying mangrove swamp. The east has savanna and there are several offshore islands. The main exports are cashews, fish and peanuts.

Bissau

Bissau, the capital, was founded in 1687 by the Portuguese as a trading post and fort on the banks of the Geba river. Fort Sao Jose was begun in 1693. It became the capital of Portuguese Guinea in 1941.

Kenya

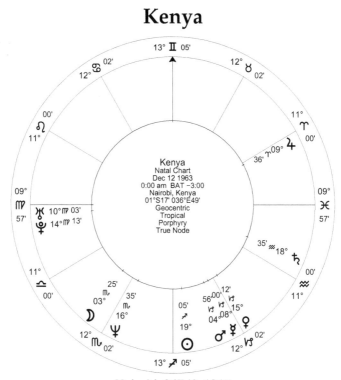

Nairobi, 36E49, 1S17
December 12, 1963, 12:00 a.m. BGT
Source: *London Times* and *Newsweek*

During the 8th century A.D., Persians and Arabs settled the coast. In 1498, Vasco da Gama arrived on his journey to India. Soon after, Portuguese traders arrived; they were expelled in 1729, most of them to Oman. In July 1895, Kenya was made a British Protectorate and a Crown Colony in July 1920. The Mau Mau revolt began in October 1952 and ended in 1959.

Independence came in December 1963 with Jomo Kenyatta as its first leader. He died in August 1978 and Daniel Arap Moi took over (progressed Sun sextile Moon conjunct Mars). He was ousted in December 2002 (progressed Sun sesquare Pluto, progressed ASC semisquare Uranus/Pluto).

Riots broke out in late December 2007 over a disputed election. Fights between various tribes ensued, killing more than 300 people, until calm was restored (progressed MC semisquare Pluto, progressed ASC conjunct Moon).

Kenya is a country of 35 million people (22 percent of them Kikiyu) living in an area the size of Texas or France. The 333 mile coastline along the Indian Ocean is lined with mangrove swamps and lagoons which abruptly rise to a plateau which ranges from 3000 to 10,000 feet.

The Great Rift Valley runs through the heart of Kenya, the highest point being Mt. Kenya (elev. 17,058 ft.). The north is semi-desert while the southwest has forests and grasslands. The main exports are coffee and tea.

Mombasa

Mombasa was founded in the 11th century by Arab traders. Shortly after Vasco da Gama visited the place on his way to India in 1498, the Portuguese arrived and took over. The British came in 1895 and started to construct a railroad to the interior of Kenya and Uganda.

Incorporated: November 1928

Nairobi

Nairobi lies 275 miles northwest of Mombasa at an elevation of 5500 feet. Its name in Masai means "cold water," or Enkare Nairobi. It was founded in June 1899 as a railroad camp along a route which would run from Mombasa to Uganda. Nairobi was made the new capital of British East Africa in 1905 (progressed MC conjunct Mercury opposition Uranus, progressed ASC sextile Jupiter) and capital of Kenya in December 1963. A university was founded here in 1956. Nairobi National Park was founded in 1946 and lies 5 miles south of the city.

Incorporated: April 1900 (municipality), March 1950 (city)

Elevation: 5500 feet

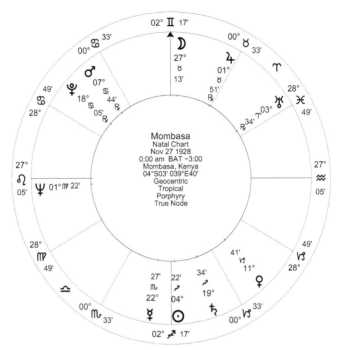

Mombasa, 39E40, 4S03
November 27, 1928, 12:00 a.m. BGT
Source: National Library of Kenya

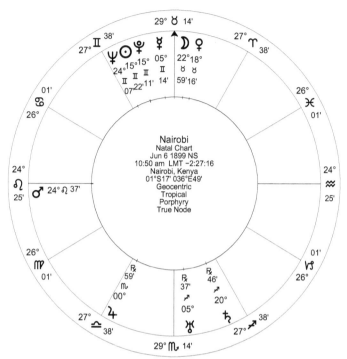

Nairobi, 36E49, 1S17
June 6, 1899, 10:50 a.m. LMT
Source: City Hall

Lesotho

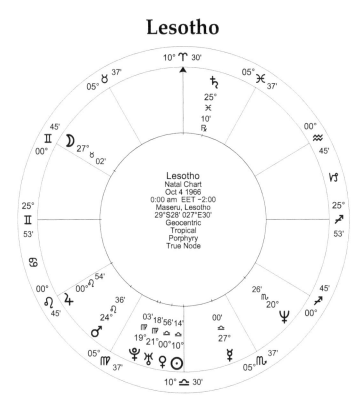

Maseru, 27E30, 29S28
October 4, 1966, 12:00 a.m. EET
Source: *London Times* **and** *New York Times*

In 1823, the Basotho nation was founded. It came under the jurisdiction of the Cape Colony in 1871 and achieved independence in October 1966.

Military rule commenced in 1970 and another coup in January 1986 was against the monarchy (progressed ASC semisquare Moon). The King was deposed and exiled in February 1990 (progressed MC sesquare Pluto, progressed Sun semisquare Pluto). Military rule ended in April 1993 (progressed MC sesquare Uranus, progressed ASC sextile Pluto, progressed Sun semisquare Uranus). The King was reinstated in January 1995 but died one year later (progressed ASC sextile Uranus).

Lesotho has two million people living in an area the size of Maryland or Belgium. The eastern part of the country is part of the Drakensberg which rises to more than 11,000 feet at Thebana. The western part are lowlands, grasslands and the Orange River valley. The main source of income are remittances sent home from South African mine workers. Over 30 percent of the adult population has AIDS. The capital is Maseru.

Liberia

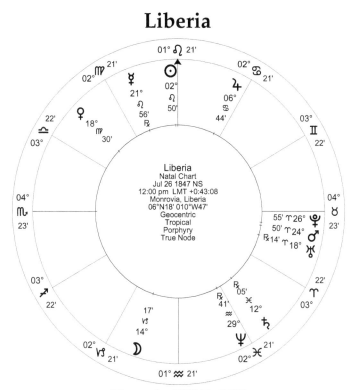

Monrovia, 10W47, 6N18
July 26, 1847, 12:00 p.m. LMT
Source: The Liberian Embassy

Portuguese explorers arrived in 1461 but had no long-lasting effect or ambitions. The American Colonization Society was formed in 1816 to resettle American slaves back to their homeland of Africa. The first settlers arrived in Monrovia in 1822 and Liberia became the first independent nation in Africa in July 1847.

William Tubman became President of Liberia in 1944 and ruled until 1971 (progressed MC trine Sun sesquare Uranus, progressed ASC sextile Pluto), when William Tolbert took over. Tolbert was killed in April 1980 (progressed MC square Saturn sesquare Pluto, progressed Sun sesquare Pluto) and Samuel Doe became Presi-

73

dent. In December 1989, an invasion led by Charles Taylor took place (progressed MC trine Mercury) and in September 1990, Samuel Doe was assassinated beginning a civil war which left 150,000 dead (progressed ASC inconjunct Mercury). The war ended in September 1996 and Charles Taylor took over in July 1997 (progressed MC sextile Neptune, progressed Sun inconjunct Sun). Taylor himself was booted out and exiled in August 2003 (progressed MC sesquare Mercury opposition Jupiter, progressed ASC sesquare Mercury, progressed Sun opposition Jupiter)\ and fled to Nigeria. Taylor is currently being tried in the Hague for war crimes (progressed MC equals Mercury/Neptune).

Liberia is a nation of 3.5 million people living in an area the size of Pennsylvania or Bulgaria. The narrow coastal plain is lined with mangrove swamps which rise to an interior plateau. Over 40 percent of the country is forested and the coastline is 360 miles long. The main exports are rubber, cocoa and coffee. One-sixth of the world's ships fly the Liberian flag. Liberia is also the world's largest exporter of iron ore.

Monrovia

Monrovia was founded in January 1822 by the American Colonization Society as a home for freed slaves. The original settlement was moved three months later (progressed Moon opposition Sun) to Providence Island at the mouth of the Mesurado river. Slaves from America began to arrive in 1830 (progressed MC square Mars, progressed ASC conjunct Venus sextile Uranus and Neptune. A university was founded in 1851 (progressed ASC conjunct Pluto) and two decades later, slaves from America stopped coming.

The port was completed in 1948 and during the civil wars of the 1990s, much of the city lay in ruins.

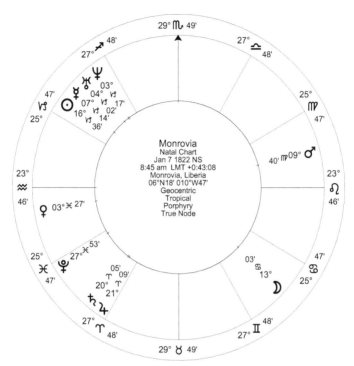

Monrovia, 10W47, 6N18
January 7, 1822, 8:45 a.m. LMT
Source: Embassy of Liberia

Libya

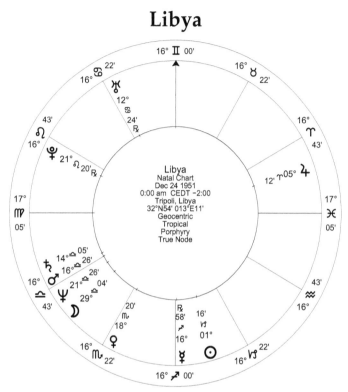

Tripoli, 13E11, 32N54
December 24, 1951, 12:00 a.m. MEDT
Source. *Le Monde*

Beginning in the 7th century B.C., this region was settled by the Phoenicians, Greeks, Carthaginians and Romans. During the 4th century A.D., it fell to the Byzantine Empire. The Arabs invaded in 642 A.D. and the Ottomans ruled from 1517. During the 19th century, it was a center for the Barbary pirates.

Italian occupation began in September 1911. During World War II, German and Italian troops were finally expelled in 1943. After the war, Britain and France ruled the region until independence came in December 1951. King Idris was the Head of State and oil was discovered in 1959.

Col. Moamar Qaddafi took over during a coup in September 1969 whereby the King was deposed (progressed MC square Jupiter, progressed ASC square Jupiter). Qaddafi then became famous for sponsoring terrorist groups and activities. In April 1986, the US bombed Tripoli and Benghazi (progressed MC square Neptune) and in December 1988, Libya was accused of complicity in the bombing of a Pan Am plane over Lockerbie, Scotland (progressed ASC conjunct Neptune sextile Pluto). In December 2003 Libya stopped nuclear development and renounced terrorism (progressed ASC inconjunct Jupiter). In October 2004, the European Union and the United Nations lifted sanctions on Libya.

Libya is a country of 6 million people (almost all of them Arab and Moslem) living in an area three times the size of France or one-sixth larger than Alaska. A narrow coastal plain fronts the Mediterranean and over 90 percent of the country is part of the Sahara. The coastline is 1100 miles long. Oil is the main export.

Tripoli

Tripoli means "three cities" which were Leptis Magna, Sabratha and Oea the forerunner of Tripoli. The original settlements were made around 500 B.C. by the Phoenicians but the area was really developed by the Romans after 146 B.C. when they conquered the region. Byzantine occupation began in the 6th century A.D. and the Arabs arrived in 645 A.D. Ottoman occupation began in 1551.

Tripoli was ruled from Italy between 1911 and 1943. During World War II it was heavily bombed.

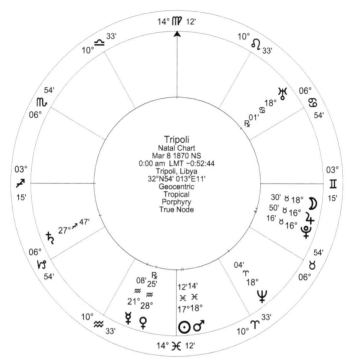

Tripoli, 13E11, 32N54
March 8, 1870, 12:00 a.m. LMT
Source: City Hall

Madagascar

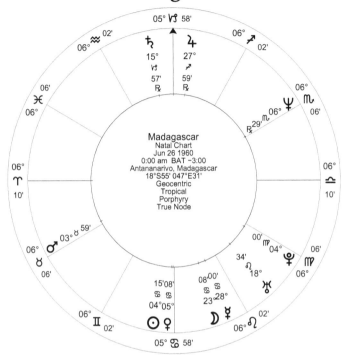

Antananarivo, 47E31, 18S55
June 26, 1960, 12:00 a.m. BGT
Source: *New York Times, New York Herald-Tribune* and *San Fran-*

During the 1st century A.D., this island was settled by Malayo-Indonesians from southeast Asia. The coastal regions were settled by Africans and Arabians. The Portuguese attempted, but failed, to colonize in the 16th century and in 1896, it became a French colony.

Independence came in June 1960 as the Malagasy Republic. An army coup occurred in 1972 against French domination (progressed MC conjunct Saturn, progressed ASC trine Uranus sesquare Pluto, progressed Sun opposition Saturn). The island was renamed in 1975 (progressed MC sesquare Pluto, progressed Sun sesquare Pluto).

Madagascar's 18 million people live on an island the size of the Ukraine or Texas. It's the world's fourth-largest island. The east side of the island is a narrow coastal plain while the west side has a broad coastal area. In the center is a plateau and highlands. The coastline is more than 3,000 miles long. The main exports are coffee and cloves. Madagascar also produces two-thirds of the world's supply of vanilla.

Antananarivo

Antananarivo, the capital, was founded in the 17th century on the Ikopa river flood plain. Imerina Kings captured the city, then known as Tananarive, in 1794. The French came in 1895 and a University was founded in 1961.

Malawi

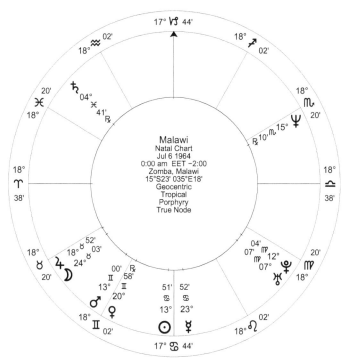

Zomba, 35E18, 15S23
July 6, 1964, 12:00 a.m. EET
Sources: *London Times*, *New York Times* and *Los Angeles Times*

During the 13th century, the Bantus arrived. David Livingstone came exploring in 1859. In May 1891, this region became the British Protectorate of Nyasaland and from October 1953 until January 1964 was part of the Federation of Rhodesia and Nyasaland.

Independence came in July 1964 with Hastings Banda as its first leader. Banda was defeated in May 1994 (progressed MC square Neptune, progressed ASC opposition Neptune, progressed Sun sextile Mars).

Malawi has 12 million people living in a area the size of Louisiana or Bulgaria. The heart of the country is the Great Rift Valley in which Lake Malawt lies. Most of the nation is a high plateau upon which grasslands and savanna predominate. The main exports are tobacco, tea, sugar and cotton.

Blantyre

Blantyre, the largest city, was founded in 1876 by Scottish missionaries and named for the birthplace of David Livingstone, the explorer.

Lilongwe

Lilongwe was chosen to be the site of the capital in 1965 by President Hastings Banda. A decade later, the government moved here from Zomba.

Mali

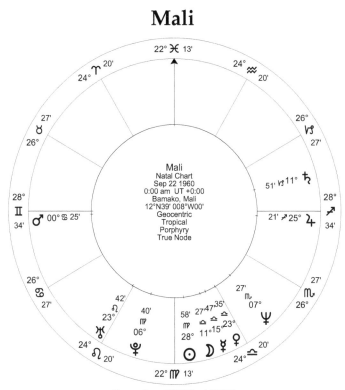

Bamako, 8W00, 12N39
September 22, 1960, l2:00 a.m. GMT
Source: *Los Angeles Times*

The Niger River civilization was founded about 200 B.C. From 750 A.D. it was part of the Ghana Empire, then the Mali Empire from the 13th-15th century and followed by the Songhai Empire in the 15th century. The heart of the latter civilizations was the famed city of Timbuktu. The French began their occupation in 1895 and Mali became the colony of the French Sudan in 1898.

Independence came in June 1960 as the Mali Federation with Senegal which seceded three months later in September 1960. In 1968, an army coup ousted Keita and replaced the leadership with Moussa Iraore (progressed MC square Mars opposition Sun, progressed ASC sextile Pluto). In March 1991, Traore himself was thrown out in another army coup (progressed MC opposition Venus trine Uranus, progressed ASC square Venus, progressed Sun trine Mars).

Mali is a land of 13 million people living in an area three times of California or twice the size of the Ukraine. Over 70 percent is a high and flat desert, a part of the Sahara. In the center are grasslands and the Sahel; the south has savanna. Mali is the source of the Senegal and Niger rivers. The main exports are cotton, peanuts and sugar.

Bamako

Bamako, the capital of Mali, was occupied by General Gallieni in 1880. A railroad to Dakar was completed in 1904; four years later Bamako became capital of the French Sudan.

Timbuktu

Timbuktu was founded in the 12th century by Tuaregs on the edge of the Sahara desert near the Niger river. Around 1200, it became a hub for the trading of gold, ivory and salt. Tribal wars during the 16th century caused the city to decline after Morocco captured Timbuktu in 1591. Previously, the place had been a major Islamic center of culture with a university and over 100 schools. Rene Caille rediscovered the city in 1828 and the French began to occupy the surrounding region in 1894.

Mauritania

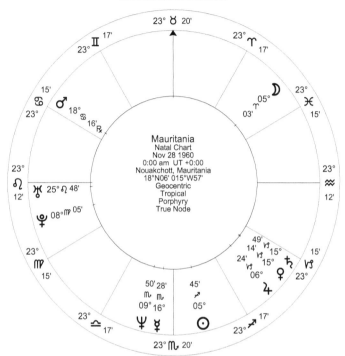

Nouakchott, 15W57, 18N06
November 28, 1960, 12:00 a.m. GMT
Source: *Los Angeles Times*

Between the 9th and 16th centuries A.D., this region was part of the Ghana, Mali and Songhai empires. Portuguese explorers arrived in the 1440s. In the 17th century it was the center for the gum arabic trade with British, French and Dutch posts. In 1903, Mauritania was made a French Protectorate and in 1920 it became a French colony.

Independence came in late November 1960. In April 1976, Spain was thrown out of Western Sahara; Morocco took the northern part, while Mauritania took the southern third (progressed MC inconjunct Neptune, progressed ASC conjunct Pluto). In 1980,

Mauritania withdrew from Western Sahara (progressed Sun trine Uranus).

A military coup in 1984 put Taya in power (progressed MC inconjunct Mercury, progressed ASC sextile Mercury). A border war erupted with Senegal in 1989 (progressed Sun square Moon conjunct Jupiter) and Taya was thrown out in August 2005 (progressed MC semisquare Uranus trine Neptune, progressed ASC semisquare Uranus).

Mauritania is a country of three million people living in an area twice the size of Spain. The north is part of the Sahara while the south is savanna. The center is a flat and rocky plateau, The coastline is 469 miles long along the Atlantic. The main exports are fish and iron ore.

Nouakchott

Nouakchott, the capital, was founded during the 1950s. Two decades later, it became a tent city for 300,000 seeking refuge from starvation during a drought. A university was opened in 1981 and a deep-water harbor was completed five years later.

Mauritius

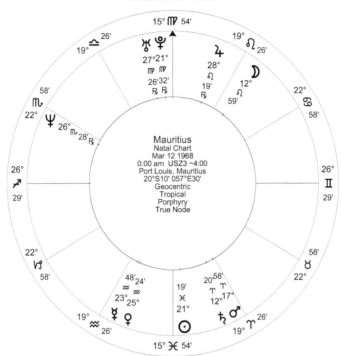

Port Louis, 57E30, 20S10
March 12, 1968, 12:00 a.m.
Source: *Los Angeles Times*

Malay sailors reached these islands in the 15th century A.D. as did Portuguese sailors by the early 16th century. The Dutch began to settle Mauritius in 1598 and held it until 1710. The French took over in 1722 but the British hcld sway after 1810. In 1834, slavery ended and laborers from India were brought in to fill the void. Independence was achieved in March 1968.

Mauritius is a series of eight volcanic islands surrounded by coral reefs about 500 miles east of Madagascar in the Indian Ocean. Its 1.3 million people live on 789 square miles, slightly smaller than Rhode Island or Luxemburg. The main exports are textiles and sugar.

Morocco

During ancient times, this region of northwest Africa was initially occupied by the Carthaginians from what-is-now Tunisia. The Romans took over after conquering Carthage in 40 B.C. Then came the Arabs who brought Islam with them in 682 A.D. During the 11th and 12th centuries, Berbers ruled the region from their headquarters across the Straits of Gibraltar in neighboring Spain. By the beginning of the 20th century, both Spain and France had their eyes on the region. France assumed a Protectorate in March 1912.

The French signed a Protocol in Paris on March 2, 1956 that agreed to pull French troops out of Morocco. This was synonymous with a Declaration of Independence. At least, that's the way Moroccans see it.

Despite what Nicholas Campion says in his book, the fact of the matter is that the date he gives for the ratification of that Protocol of May 28, 1956 at 11:00 a.m. GMT in Rabat (or noon in Paris) just doesn't work for me, using either transits or progressions.

The Spanish ceded their territory in the north on April 7, and Morocco became a member of the United Nations on April 22, 1956. The region around Tangier became a part of Morocco on October 29. The region of Ifni was assimilated in 1969.

The monarchy was established in August 1957 (progressed ASC trine Venus sextile Jupiter, progressed Sun sesquare Uranus). The king, however, died in February 1961 (progressed ASC sextile Pluto). A state of emergency had been declared twice, in both 1965 (progressed MC trine Sun, progressed ASC trine Neptune) and 1970 (progressed Sun inconjunct Pluto). Between these dates, the progressed ASC was also opposition natal Mars. When the Spanish pulled out of Western Sahara in Anril 1976, Morocco waltzed in and occupied the region (progressed ASC semisquare Jupiter, progressed Sun semisquare Mercury square Mars).

A treaty with the Polisaro rebels was signed in 1979 (progressed ASC trine Sun semisquare Pluto, progressed Sun sesquare

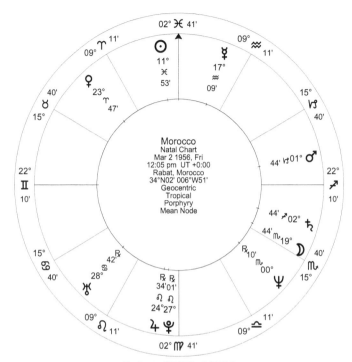

Rabat, 6W51, 34N02
March 2, 1956, 12:05 p.m. GMT
Source: Author's rectification

Moon). A sandwall around western Sahara was begun in April 1987 (progressed MC trine Saturn, progressed ASC inconjunct Mercury sesquare Saturn, progressed Sun sesquare Pluto).

A general strike across the country came to pass in 1991 (progressed Sun sextile Mercury sesquare Saturn). The King died in July 1999 (progressed ASC sesquare Sun, progressed Sun conjunct Venus trine Jupiter). Suicide bombings in the city of Casablanca in May 2003 caused extensive damage and killed many (progressed MC inconjunct Moon, progressed ASC square Neptune, progressed Sun square Uranus).

Morocco is a nation of 33 million people living in an area the size of California or Sweden. A narrow coastal plain along the Atlantic Ocean yields to three ranges of the Atlas Mountains. The Sahara occupies most of the eastern part of Morocco. The coastline along the Atlantic and Mediterranean is 1140 miles long. The highest point is Djebel Taubkal (elev. 13,665 ft.) The chief exports are phosphates (the world's third-largest exporter) and foodstuffs.

Note: Morocco also controls Western Sahara, a former Spanish enclave of 103,000 square miles with a population of about 275,000 people. The coastline is 690 miles long and the main export is phosphates.

Casablanca

This city sits on the Atlantic about 60 miles south of the capital, Rabat. It handles over 75 percent of Morocco's foreign trade. During the 12th century, a village called Anfa was founded, and the Portuguese destroyed it in 1468. A new city called Casa Branca was founded in 1515 by the Portuguese, but it was largely destroyed by the earthquake of November 1755 which also wrecked Lisbon. Casablanca is home to one of the world's largest temples of worship, the Hassan II Mosque, built over the water.

Fes

Fes was founded in 789 A.D on both banks of the Wadi Fes. It became a cultural and spiritual capital and one of the sacred cities of Islam. In 809 A.D., Fes was chosen by Idriss II as his capital and by 859 A.D., a University was founded, one of the oldest in the world. Fes reached its zenith during the 14th century. The city has many mosques, shrines, colleges, palaces and markets. It also has the largest Medina in Morocco as well as the Qaraouyine Mosque, one of the largest in Islam.

Marrakesh

Marrakesh lies at the foot of the Atlas Mountains. It was founded in 1062 A.D. by Yusuf ibn Tashufin. The city was captured by the Almoravid dynasty in 1147 but fell to Marinid control in 1265.

Rabat

Rabat lies on the Bou Regreg river where it empties into the Atlantic some 55 miles from Casablanca. Its name means "camp" in Arabic. Rabat was founded in 1146 by Abd al Mumin, first ruler of the Almohad dynasty. In 1609, neighboring Sale became home to Andalusian Moors escaping from Spain. In 1913, the capital was moved from Fes to Rabat. Mohammed V University opened in 1957. Outside the city is the old Roman town of Chella.

Tangier

Tangier was founded by the Phoenicians in the 5th century B.C. It was then occupied by Carthaginians, and next by the Romans who named it Tingis in 42 A.D. Tangier became the capital of the Roman province of Mauretania.

Vandals in the 5th century A.D., and the Arabs invaded in 705 A.D. The Spanish and Portuguese ruled from 1471 to 1662, when the British took over. Tangier lies only 17 miles from Spain at the western end of the Mediterranean Sea was granted special status in 1912, separate from the rest of Morocco. It became an international city, one of spies and intrigue, from 1923 until 1956 when Morocco gained its independence from France. The American University was founded in 1968 and the University of North Africa opened its doors in 1971.

Mozambique

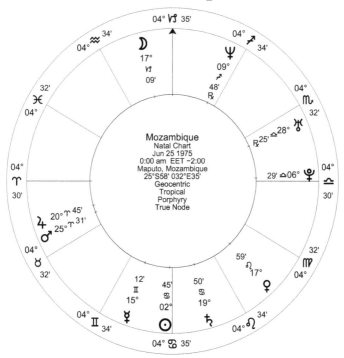

Maputo, 32E35, 25858
June 25, 1975 12:00 a.m. EET
Source: CBS

Arab traders plied the region during the 9th century A.D. Portuguese trading posts were built beginning in 1505 in their hunt for gold, ivory and slaves. In 1885, Mozambique became a Portuguese colony. FRELIMO was founded in 1961 to attain independence and a guerrilla war began. That freedom came in late June 1975. Samora Michel became its first leader but his Marxist policies caused most of the white people to leave.

A civil war erupted in 1980 (progressed ASC trine Neptune, progressed Sun square Pluto) and ended in 1989 with Samora Michel's death and FRELIMO's dropping a Communist policy (progressed MC inconjunct Venus, progressed ASC square Moon, progressed Sun opposition Moon). Massive floods in 1989 left over 200,000 stranded and homeless. A severe drought in 1992 caused more than two million to depend on outside aid (progressed MC square Jupiter opposition Saturn, progressed ASC conjunct Jupiter square Saturn). Further floods in March 2000 displaced more than one million people (progressed MC square Uranus, progressed ASC opposition Uranus, progressed Sun square Mars).

Mozambique is a country of 20 million people living in an area twice the size of California or three times the size of the United Kingdom. The 1535 mile long coastline has dunes, swamps and offshore reefs. In the center are plateaus, highlands and mountains. The chief exports are shrimp, cashews, sugar and cotton. About 12 percent of the adult population has AIDS.

Maputo

Maputo was founded in November 1781 as a military trading post. Originally called Lourenco Marques, it's located on Espiritu Santo estuary of Delagoa Bay. The fort was dedicated in April 1782 but was burned one month later (progressed Moon opposition Neptune, progressed Mars conjunct ASC). The place was abandoned in 1783 (progressed MC inconjunct Uranus trine Moon) but was reoccupied one year later. The French looted and burned the town in 1796 (progressed ASC sextile Venus).

A railroad was built to Pretoria in 1883 (progressed ASC opposition Jupiter) and to Johannesburg twelve years later. Lourenco Marques became the capital of Mozambique in 1907 (progressed MC trine Jupiter). A University was founded in 1962 (progressed MC square Mars sextile Moon, progressed ASC trine Saturn) and its name was changed to Maputo one year after Mozambique achieved its independence from Portugal in 1976 (progressed ASC square Jupiter).

Incorporated: November 1887

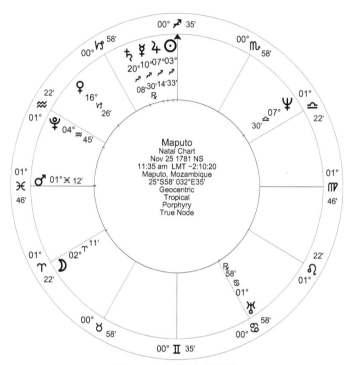

Maputo, 32E35, 25S58
November 25, 1781, 11:35 a.m. LMT
Source: City Hall

Namibia

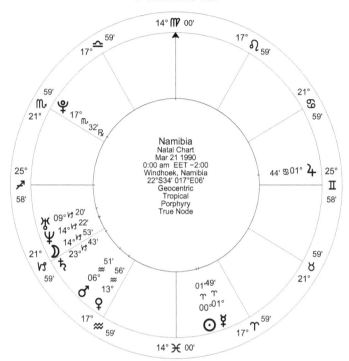

Windhoek, 17E06, 22S34
March 21, 1990, 12:00 a.m. EET
Source: BBC and *The Guardian*

In ancient times, this was the land of the Bushmen and Hottentots. The British established a post at Walvis Bay in 1872 and by April 1884, the Germans occupied the region. They founded a Protectorate in 1890. In 1915, South African occupation began, and the region was known as South West Africa. South Africa was given a mandate over this territory in May 1919 which lasted until 1966. SWAPO fomented a civil war that same year and the International Court of Justice ruled in 1971 that further South African rule was illegal. A cease-fire was promulgated in 1988 between South Africa, Angola and Cuba.

Independence came in March 1990 and the British handed over Walvis Bay in March 1994 (progressed MC sextile Pluto, progressed ASC square Sun semisquare Venus).

Namibia's two million people live in an area the size of Turkey or twice the area of California. The coastline (976 miles long) is part of the Namib desert while most of the rest of the country is part of the vast Kalahari desert. A high plateau in the center is largely grassland or scrub. The main exports are diamonds, uranium, gold, zinc, copper and lead.

Windhoek

Windhoek was founded in October 1890 by the Germans and became the capital of German Southwest Africa. The nation of

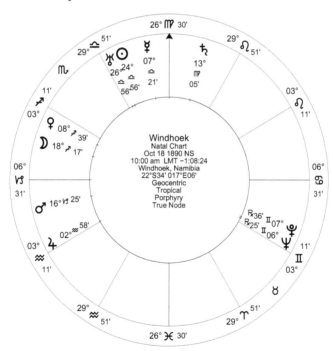

Windhoek, 17E06, 22S34
October 18, 1890, 10:00 a.m. LMT
Source: Internet

South Africa occupied the region in 1915 during the early days of World War I (progressed MC sesquare Neptune and Pluto, progressed ASC square Uranus).

Niger

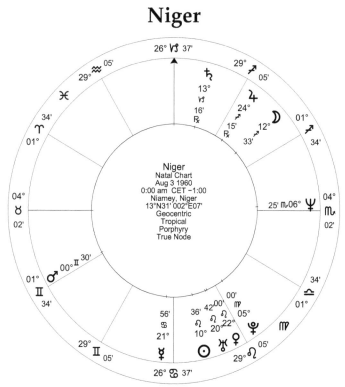

Niamey, 2E07, 13N31
August 3, 1960, 12:00 a.m. MET
Source: *Los Angeles Times*

Around 1000 A.D., the Tuaregs settled this region and in the 15th century, Niger became part of the Songhai Empire, and in 1904 it became part of French West Africa. It was made a French colony in 1922. Independence came in August 1960.

A military coup in 1974 ousted Hamani Diori (progressed MC opposition Sun semisquare Jupiter, progressed ASC square Uranus, progressed Sun trine Jupiter). Civilian rule returned in 1989 (progressed MC sextile Jupiter, progressed ASC square Pluto, progressed Sun semisquare Mercury). The Tuaregs rebelled between 1990 and 1995.

Another military coup took place in January 1996 and both the president and prime minister were ousted (progressed MC square Mars, progressed ASC sextile Sun, progressed Sun trine Saturn). The President, Ibrahim Barre, was assassinated in April 1999 (progressed MC opposition Pluto, progressed ASC opposition Moon inconjunct Saturn).

Niger has 12 million people living in a region twice the size of the Ukraine or three times the area of California. The Sahara occupies the northern tier while the Sahel and savanna dominate the south.

In the southeast is the Lake Chad basin and in the southwest is the source of the Niger river. Main exports are uranium (world's number four), peanuts and cotton.

Niamey

Niamey, the capital, was probably founded in the 18th century. It was still a small village when the French colonized the region in 1890. A fort was constructed in 1902 and Niamey became the capital in 1927. A university was established in 1971.

Nigeria

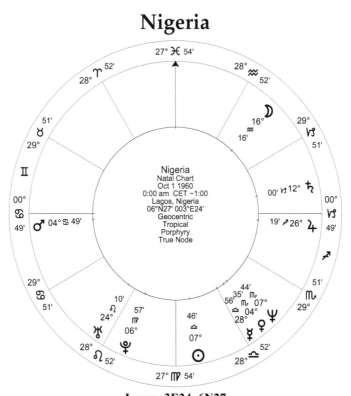

Lagos, 3E24, 6N27
October 1, 1960 12:00 a.m. MET
Source: *New York Times* and *London Times*

In ancient times, this was the land of the Nok civilization which existed until 200 B.C. Then followed the Ibo and Yoruba civilizations until the 14th century. At that time, northern Nigeria was part of the Kanem-Bornu Empire while in the 15th century A.D., the Hausa-Songhai Empire was overthrown by the Fulanis. From the 16th to 18th century, Nigeria was part of the Benin civilization.

Portuguese trading stations were set up during the 15th century and Nigeria became a center for the slave trade. By the end of the 18th century, most of the coast was under British control. The British occupied Lagos in late December 1851 and ten years later, Nigeria was made a British colony. Southern and Northern Nigeria was founded in January 1900.

Independence came from Britain in October 1960 and ethnic rivalry ensued over political dominance. An Ibo army coup erupted in January 1966 (progressed MC square Mars, progressed Sun square Saturn) and a civil war followed; Aguiyi-Ironsi was assassinated and Yakubu Gowon was sworn in in July 1966. The following year, Nigeria was reapportioned into 12 states and Biafra decided to secede in May 1967 and another civil war broke out (progressed MC inconjunct Venus, progressed ASC square Sun trine Neptune sextile Pluto). When the war in Biafra ended in January 1970, more than one million had been killed (progressed MC opposition Sun inconjunct Neptune and Pluto, progressed ASC semisquare Uranus, progressed Sun trine Moon). Gowon was thrown out in 1975 (progressed MC square Saturn progressed ASC opposition Saturn, progressed Sun semisquare Pluto).

Civilian rule returned in October 1979 (progressed MC sextile Moon, progressed ASC inconjunct Moon, progressed Sun sextile Jupiter). Military rule again returned in December 1983 (progressed MC sesquare Pluto). Religious violence erupted between Christians and Moslems in 1987 (progressed MC trine Uranus, progressed ASC semisquare Pluto, progressed Sun conjunct Venus trine Mars). Another military coup took place in November 1993 and Sani Abacha was sworn in (progressed ASC square Mercury, progressed Sun semisquare Jupiter), Abacha died in June 1998 (progressed MC opposition Venus sextile Mars, progressed ASC square Venus, progressed Sun square Moon). By July 2000, the rush towards Sharia law provoked further clashes between Moslem and Christian groups (progressed MC inconjunct Sun opposition Neptune trine Pluto).

Population: 130 million, the most populous nation in Africa, 29% Hausa, 21% Yoruba, 18% Ibo, 11% Fulani

Religion: 50% Moslem, 40% Christian

Area: 357,000 square miles (three times the size of Arizona or twice the size of Sweden)

Geography: In the north is a desert, the northeast high plains and savanna sitting on a plateau. In the center is a rainforest and the south has broad coastal plains and mangrove swamps. Nigeria is the mouth of the Niger river and its delta. The coastline is 530 miles long and the highest point is Vogel Peak (6700 ft.).

Economy: Nigeria is a member of OPEC and its main export is oil. Then comes cocoa and rubber.

Abuja

Abuja, the present capital, is located in the Chukuku hills about 325 miles northeast of Lagos. It became the capital of Nigeria on December 12, 1991.

Lagos

Lagos, the original capital, was founded on an island in the 13th century by the Yorubas. The Portuguese began to settle the region in 1472. The British arrived in late December 1851 and assumed control of the country a decade later. Lagos became the capital in 1914. A university was founded in 1962.

Two bridges link the island of Lagos to the mainland. The city consists of four main islands, the highest point being only 22 feet. Most of the population lives in overcrowded squalid slums with open sewers. Lagos is one of the largest cities in Africa. with a population of anywhere from 9 to 16 million struggling to survive in a sea of chaos, noise and confusion.

Rwanda

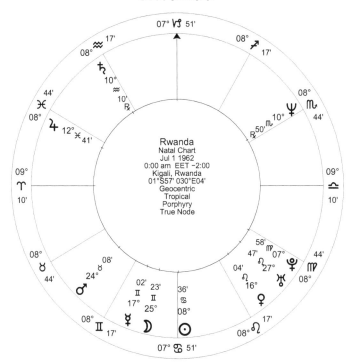

Kigali, 30E04, lS57
July 1, 1962 l2:00 a.m. BET
Source: New York Times and Le Soir

Around 1000 A.D., the Hutus began to replace the Twa people. The Tutsi tribe began to dominate during the 15th century. German occupation began in 1899—the region was known as Ruanda-Urundi. During World War I, Belgian occupation took over in 1916. In 1959, a Hutu rebellion ended Tutsi power.

Independence came in July 1962 and another brief rebellion erupted. But the real and bloody civil war erupted in April 1994 when the Presidents of both Rwanda and Burundi were killed in a plane crash (progressed MC inconjunct Sun and Pluto, progressed ASC sextile Jupiter, progressed Sun square Neptune). More than one million were massacred and three million were exiled or fled the country. United Nations troops left in March 1996 but by October 1996, Rwanda was at war with Zaire over refugees in their territory (progressed Me conjunct Saturn square Neptune, progressed Sun semisquare Moon opposition Saturn). By 1998, the courts had executed 22 individuals for genocide (progressed ASC square Venus). In 2000, the first Tutsi President was elected (progressed Sun square Venus).

Rwanda is a country of 8.5 million people living in an area the size of Maryland or Albania. It's the most densely-packed nation in Africa. The chief feature of Rwanda is the Great Rift Valley. In the northwest are volcanic mountains and the eastern part has plateaus. The highest point is Karisimbi (elev. 14,780 ft.). The main exports are coffee and tea.

Kigali

Kigali, the capital, was founded by Germans in 1907. It suffered catastrophic damage during the civil war of 1994 and much of the city lay in ruins.

Sao Tome and Principe

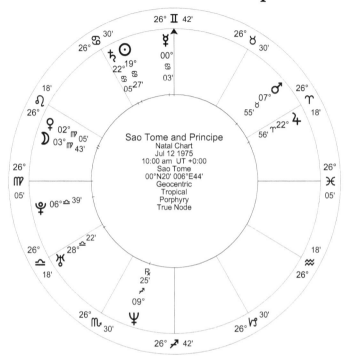

Sao Tome, 6E44, 0N20
July 12, 1975, 10:00 a.m. GMT
Source: *Le Soir*; *San Francisco Chronicle*
and ABC indicate "midnight" or 12:00 a.m.

The Portuguese reached the islands in 1470. The first settlement occurred in 1522 when the slave trade began. The land was colonized by convicts and exiled Jews. Slavery was abolished in 1876 but abuses continued. Independence from Portugal came in July 1975 and a Socialist regime was instituted.

Marxism was thrown out in 1990 after the fall of Communism in eastern Europe. Sao Tome has endured two brief military coups - the one in 1990 lasted only a week (progressed MC semisquare Venus, progressed Sun square Mars) as did the brief coup in July

2003 (progressed MC square Jupiter sesquare Neptune, progressed ASC conjunct Uranus, progressed Sun semisquare Mercury).

Sao Tome has a population of about 200,000 living in 371 square miles some 125 miles out in the Atlantic Ocean west of Gabon. The country consists of two main islands, Sao Tome and Principe. It's the smallest nation in Africa. The coastline is 135 miles long. The chief exports are cocoa, copra and coffee.

Senegal

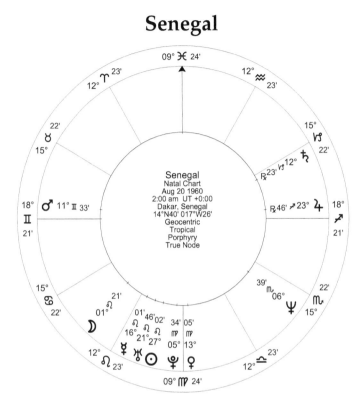

Dakar, 17W26, 14N40
August 20, 1960, 2:00 a.m. GMT
Source: *Book of World Horoscopes* by Nicholas Campion

From the 4th to the 16th century A.D., this region was part of the Empires of Ghana, Mali and Songhai. Berbers brought Islam to the area in the 14th century and Portuguese sailors arrived in 1444. The French settled Senegal in 1659 and competition between the British, French and Dutch for slaves was intense.

In 1765, the British established Senegambia but ceded the region to France in 1783. Senegal was created a French colony in 1882 and part of French West Africa in 1895. The Federation of Mali was founded in 1959 but fell apart when Senegal decided to go its own way in August 1960. Leopold Senghor was its first leader.

Senghor retired in 1981 (progressed ASC trine Neptune, progressed Sun semisquare Moon) and was succeeded by Abdou Diouf. Another confederation of Senegambia existed again between 1982 until it broke up in 1989 (progressed MC semisquare Uranus, progressed ASC sextile Venus opposition Saturn).

Senegal is a land of 11 million people living in an area the size of Nebraska or Belarus. Low plains and sand dunes dominate the north, in the center are grasslands and scrub while the south is covered by Savanna. The coastline is 330 miles long. Senegal is the westernmost country on the continent of Africa. The main exports are fish, peanuts, phosphates and cotton. Oil refining is the chief industry, however.

Dakar

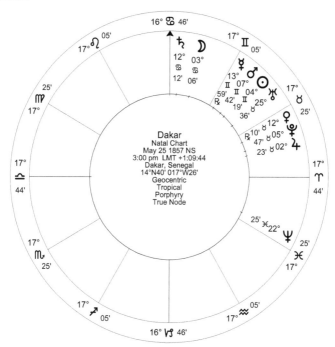

Dakar, 17W26, 14N40
May 25, 1857, 3:00 p.m. LMT
Source: Archives du Senegal

The settlement on the island of Goree was founded by the Dutch in 1617. It was captured by the French six decades later. The present city of Dakar was founded by the French as a fort in May 1857. The first ships left for South America nine years later (progressed MC sextile Uranus). A railroad was completed to St. Louis in 1885 (progressed MC sextile Mercury), a breakwater was completed in 1892 and a naval base established in 1898 (progressed MC square Uranus). In 1904. Dakar became the capital of French West Africa (progressed MC trine Jupiter), and of Senegal in 1958. The airport opened in 1943 (progressed ASC trine Jupiter opposition Moon) a major transit station for those flying from Europe to South America.

Seychelles

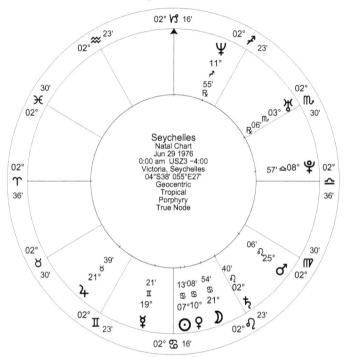

Victoria, 55E27, 4S38
June 29, 1076, 12:00 a.m.
Source: *San Francisco Examiner* and CBS

The French occupied these islands in 1768 but were forced to leave by the British who captured the region in 1794. The Seychelles were ruled from Mauritius beginning in 1814 but by 1903, the islands were made a separate colony.

Independence came in June 1976. The following year, a socialist coup removed the President from office (progressed MC inconjunct Saturn, progressed ASC inconjunct Uranus, progressed Sun square Pluto).

The Seychelles consist of four large islands and 86 smaller islets in the Indian Ocean some 700 miles northeast of Madagascar and about 1000 miles east of Kenya. The coastline is 305 miles long. The chief exports are fish, cinnamon and copra. Tourism is the mainstay of the economy, however.

Sierra Leone

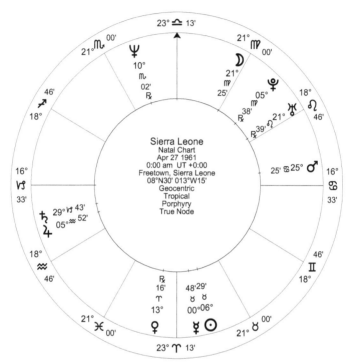

Freetown, 13W15, 8N30
April 27, 1961, 12:00 a.m. GMT
Source: *New York Times* and *London Times*

Portuguese sailors arrived on the scene in 1462 and gave the region its name, Sierra Leoa, or mountain lion. The slave trade began in the 16th century and Freetown was settled in 1787 as a haven for freed slaves from Great Britain, the United States and the Caribbean. Sierra Leone was made a British colony in 1808; in August 1896 it became a British Protectorate.

Independence came in April 1961. A military coup toppled the government in 1968 (pr MC conj Mercury). A civil war broke out in 1991 (progressed MC sextile Moon square Uranus, progressed Sun square Pluto) which led to another coup in April 1992 (progressed Sun trine Jupiter). Liberia invaded Freetown in 1999 (progressed MC inconjunct Mercury sextile Saturn, progressed ASC opposition Moon/Mars, progressed Sun square Moon/Pluto sesquare Saturn). The civil war officially ended in May 2000 when the rebel leader, Foday Sankoh, was captured. In January 2002, the United Nations set up a war crimes tribunal and invoked pleas for disarmament (progressed ASC inconjunct Mars, progressed Sun semisquare Mercury).

Sierra Leone is a country of six million people living in an area the size of West Virginia or Ireland. The coastal plain rises to a plateau and then mountains. The coastline is 250 miles long and has numerous lagoons and swamps. The north is savanna country.

The main exports are diamonds (world's number nine), bauxite and rutile. Coffee and cocoa are also exported.

Freetown

Freetown was founded in May 1787 on the banks of the Sierra Leone river by Granville Sharp as a settlement for freed slaves from Great Britain, Nova Scotia and Jamaica, among others. It was sacked by the French in 1794 (progressed MC semisquare Mercury sesquare Uranus). Beginning in 1808, Freetown was a base for slave patrols and suppression of the slave trade.

By 1821, Freetown had become the capital of all British possessions in West Africa (progressed MC conjunct Mars). In 1898, it was made capital of Sierra Leone (progressed MC trine Neptune and Pluto).

In 1999, the rebels from neighboring Liberia invaded the city (progressed MC inconjunct Saturn, progressed Sun sextile Neptune and Pluto). The scale of the atrocities were unmatched in recent history: burning, kill mg, amputations, abductions, looting and considerable abuse of women.

Incorporated: 1893

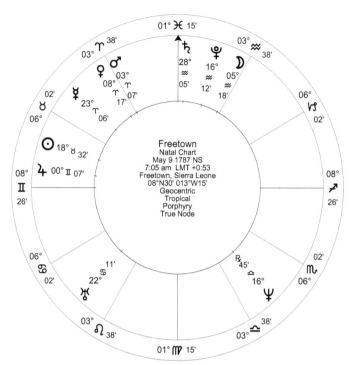

Freetown, 13W15, 8N30
May 9, 1787, 7:05 am. LMT
Source: City Hall

Somalia

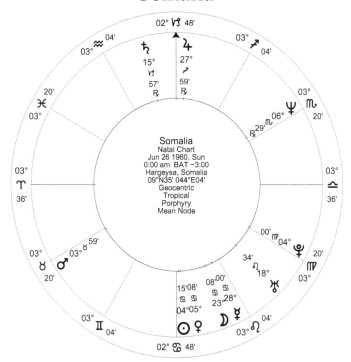

Hargeysa, 44E05, 9N35
June 26, 1960, 12:00 a.m. BGT
Source: *London Times* **and** *The Guardian*

Arabs began to settle the coast during the 7th century A.D. and the Portuguese arrived in the 15th century. By 1840, the British occupied the north (Berbera) and by 1897, Italy occupied the south around Mogadishu. Italy invaded British Somaliland in 1940 but the following year, the British drove out the Italians and ruled the entire region until 1950. Independence came in June 1960.

A military coup led by Mohamed Barre assassinated the President in October 1969 (progressed ASC square Saturn). The new regime supported rebels in Ogaden (a region of Ethiopia) during 1977, and more than 1.5 million refugees landed in Somalia (progressed MC sesquare Pluto, progressed ASC square Moon, progressed Sun semisquare Pluto). In May 1988, a peace treaty was signed with Ethiopia (progressed ASC opposition Neptune).

In December 1990, a civil war broke out with rebels in the north who wanted to secede from the central government (progressed Sun square Mars). UN troops invaded in December 1992 during a famine in which over 300,000 died and two million refugees fled to other countries (progressed MC inconjunct Sun and Pluto square Mars). When the UN troops left in March 1995, there was no longer a central government, only clan warfare between the tribes (progressed MC square Neptune, progressed ASC sesquare Jupiter, progressed Sun square Neptune).

In August 1996, Mohamed Aidid was shot and clan warfare escalated (progressed ASC trine Saturn). Olan warlords renewed the civil war in May 2001 (progressed MC semisquare Jupiter, progressed ASC semisquare Sun, progressed Sun sesquare Jupiter). In January 2004, a transitional capital with a new Parliament was set up in Jowhar (progressed ASC sextile Moon, progressed Sun inconjunct Saturn).

Somalia has been functioning without a central government since 1991, when the country was carved up into rival fiefdoms. Plans to attack the temporary capital of Baidoa erupted in October 2006, a few months after Mogadishu was captured by the Islamic militia (progressed MC opposition Uranus).

Somalia is a land of nine million people living in an area about the size of Texas or the Ukraine. The north is mountainous while the south has low plateaus and semi-desert. The coastline along the Red Sea and the Indian Ocean is 1880 miles long. Somalia sits at the Horn of Africa, the easternmost point on the continent. Main exports are livestock, hides and skins.

Mogadishu

Mogadishu, the capital, was founded in the 10th century by Persian and Arab merchants. It was conquered by the Portuguese six centuries later and seized by the Sultan of Zanzibar in 1871. The region was sold to Italy in 1905.

During World War II, Mogadishu was taken by the British in 1941. A University was founded in 1954. When various parts of Somaliland were united in June 1960, Mogadishu became the capital. During the civil war in 1992, over 75 percent of the city lay in ruins and over 50,000 were killed.

South Africa

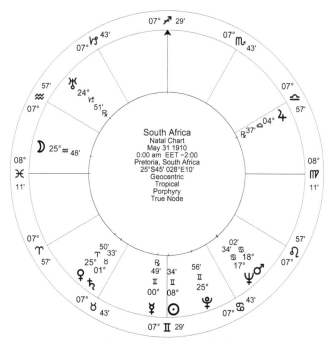

Pretoria, 28E10, 25S45
May 31, 1910, 12:00 a.m. EET
Source: *London Times* says the governor general
took the oath at noon.

In ancient times, this was the home of the Khoisan people. The Bantu people arrived about the 1st century A.D. along with the Zulu and Xhosa tribes. Bartolomeo Dias rounded the Cape of Good Hope in 1488 paving the way for Vasco da Gama to venture to India a decade later. The Dutch arrived in April 1652 and founded the city of Cape Town. The British took over in January 1806. The Great Trek by the Boers (Dutch) began in 1836 fleeing British control and the Zulu Wars began in 1838 and lasted until 1879 with the surrender of Shaka.

In 1841 the Cape Colony was founded, five years after the Orange Free State. In 1843, Natal was born and the Transvaal was born in 1848 and remained independent until April 1877 when it was annexed to Britain. The first Boer War began in 1881 and lasted one year. The Second Boer War began in October 1899 and lasted until May 1902. The Orange Free State came under British control in May 1900. All of the above provinces became the Union of South Africa when it was formed at the end of May 1910.

South Africa joined the Allies in September 1939 at the beginning of World War II (pr ASC opp Jupiter). In 1948, a new Parliament decided to adopt Apartheid (separateness of the races) as the law of the land (progressed Sun semisquare Mercury). It required that all black persons carry passes and papers and there was to be no mixing of the races. In May 1960, the Sharpeville riots protested Apartheid (progressed MC conjunct Uranus, progressed ASC semisquare Sun sesquare Uranus, progressed Sun square Venus). South Africa left the British Commonwealth in May 1961 when it became a Republic.

The Soweto riots outside Johannesburg erupted in June 1976 (progressed MC sesquare Pluto, progressed Sun semisquare Pluto). Military operations in Angola and Mozambique took place in 1981 against insurgents trying to overthrow the government (progressed ASC semisquare Pluto). A state of emergency was declared at this time. In 1985, inter-racial marriage was permitted for the first time in years (progressed MC sesquare Jupiter, progressed Sun semisquare Jupiter).

In May 1986, South African troops attacked guerrilla strongholds in Zimbabwe, Botswana and Zambia (progressed ASC sextile Neptune). Dr. Desmond Tutu asked for renewed sanctions against the government. Black workers struck against government policies in June 1988 (progressed ASC sextile Mars) and in 1990, the ban against the ANC (African National Congress) was lifted by Botha and Nelson Mandela was released from prison in February after 28 years in prison at Robben Island outside Cape Town (progressed ASC sesquare Jupiter, progressed Sun opposition Moon inconjunct Uranus). The former homelands (unrecognized by any other country) were abolished (progressed MC conjunct Moon).

The first multi-racial elections were held in April 1994—the ANC won and Nelson Mandela became President. A new Constitution was drawn up in May 1996 with basic rights given irrespective of race, creed, color, sex or sexual persuasion. South Africa had become "the Rainbow Nation" (progressed ASC square Moon, progressed Sun square Mercury trine Saturn).

South Africa became the first nation in Africa, and the fifth in the world, to legalize same-sex marriages in November 2006 (progressed MC semisquare Venus, progressed ASC trine Jupiter). The other nations legalizing same-sex marriages are the Netherlands, Belgium and Spain in Europe and Canada in the Western Hemisphere.

South Africa is a country of 45 million people of which 75 percent are black, 14 percent are white, eight percent are colored, three percent are Asian and 70 percent are Christian. They live in an area three times the area of California and twice the area of the Ukraine. The interior consists of a high plateau and the Drakensberg mountains. In the southwest are the Cape mountains and in the northwest are the Namib desert, grasslands and savanna. There is a narrow coastal plain, the coastline being 1739 miles long. South Africa is the most economically-developed country in Africa. It leads in world production of diamonds and gold. Other main exports are chromium, chemicals, iron and steel. However, on the downside, about 22 percent of the adult population has AIDS.

Bloemfontein

Bloemfontein was founded in late August 1846 by the Boers fleeing from the British by Major H. Douglas Warden. Its name means "fountain of flowers." It became the capital of the Orange Free State in 1854 (progressed MC square Jupiter, progressed ASC trine Mercury). The University of the OFS was founded the following year.

A conference between the British and the Boers (Dutch) failed to reach an agreement in May 1899 which led to the Boer War later that year (progressed MC opposition Pluto, progressed ASC semisquare Saturn and Neptune). When South Africa became a na-

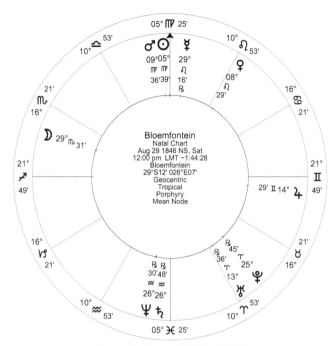

Bloemfontein, 26E07, 29S12
August 29, 1846, 12:00 p.m. LMT
Source: South Africa College of Astrology

tion in May 1910, Bloemfontein became home to the judiciary, one of the three capitals of South Africa (progressed MC square Venus sextile Sun/Mars, progressed ASC trine Jupiter sextile Uranus).

Elevation: 4570 feet
Incorporated: March 1945

Cape Town

Cape Town was founded in April 1652 by Jan van Riebeek as a supply station or refreshment station for sailors rounding the tip of Africa on their way to the riches of India and the Far East. It was under the administration of the Dutch East India Company. The Castle of Good Hope was built in 1667 (progressed MC sextile

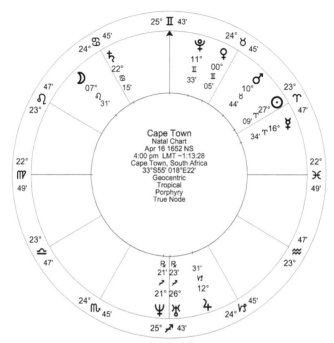

Cape Town, l8E22, 33S55
April 6, 1652 (OS) or April 16, 1652 (NS) at 4:00 p.m. LMT
Source: Suid-Afrikaanse Biblioteek

Mars, progressed ASC opposition Mercury). The British tried to occupy the region in 1781 but the French arrived first (progressed MC inconjunct Venus). The British finally succeeded in gaining control in 1795 (progressed MC sextile Jupiter) but ruled for only eight years until the Dutch regained supremacy for the next three years, until the British took over once and for all (progressed ASC sextile Sun square Venus).

In 1829, the South African College and University of Cape Town opened (progressed MC trine Mercury). A railroad to Wynberg was begun in 1859 (progressed ASC conjunct Mercury). With the opening of the Suez Canal in November 1869, the fortunes of Cape Town declined (progressed MC square Sun sesquare Pluto, progressed ASC square Saturn). Diamonds were discovered the following year (progressed MC trine Venus, progressed ASC conjunct Sun trine Uranus) and gold was discovered in the Transvaal in 1886 (progressed ASC opposition Mars).

When South Africa became a nation in May 1910, Cape Town became the legislative capital of the new nation and home to its parliament (progressed MC inconjunct Moon, progressed ASC inconjunct Uranus). In 1967, Dr. Christiaan Barnard performed the world's first heart transplant at the Groote Schuur hospital (progressed MC trine Jupiter, progressed ASC conjunct Saturn).

Cape Town is the most beautiful city on the continent. Hovering above the city is Table Mtn. (elev. 3563 ft.) which is reached by cable car. Numerous historic buildings, many from the early Dutch colonial period dot the region. Some thirty miles south of Cape Town is the Cape of Good Hope, the southernmost point of Africa.

Incorporated: 1840 (municipality), 1867 (city), 1913 (greater Cape Town)

Durban

Durban was originally settled in April 1824 as Port Natal by Francis Farewell. Its present founding dates to June 1835 when the settlement was renamed Durban to honor Benjamin D'Urban, Governor of the Cape Colony. In 1909, the University of Natal was founded (progressed MC sextile Mercury). Durban today is the largest and busiest port in Africa and a major tourist destination.

Incorporated: 1854 (borough), 1935 (city)

East London

The first settlement in November 1836 was named Port Rex at the mouth of the Buffalo river where it meets the Indian Ocean. It was annexed to the Cape Colony in 1847 and the present city was founded in January 1848.

Incorporated: 1873 (municipality), 1914 (city)

Johannesburg

Johannesburg was first settled on September 8, 1886 and three months later, in December, the first sale of lots was held. It was

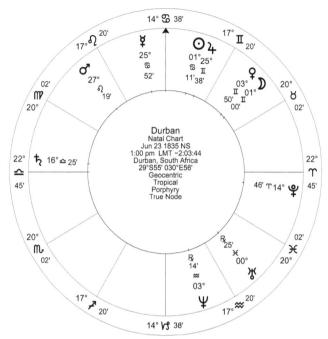

Durban, 30E56, 29S55
June 23, 1835, 1:00 p.m. LMT
Source: Stadsbibliotek

named to honor the Vice President of the Transvaal, Johannes Joubert, and the Surgeon General, Johann Rissik. The natives called the place E-Goli, or "place of gold" the mineral that gave birth to this city. Pyrite was found in 1889 thus closing the mines briefly (progressed ASC square Neptune).

A railroad to Cape Town was constructed in 1892 (progressed ASC trine Jupiter) and Johannesburg was captured during the Boer War in 1900 (progressed MC conjunct Mercury). The first Chinese settlers arrived in 1902 (progressed ASC sesquare Saturn). The University of Witwatersrand opened in 1922, the same year a massive strike caused 200 to perish (progressed MC sextile Jupiter).

Johannesburg is a tumultuous place and the crime rate is high. During the years of Apartheid, the blacks revolted numerous

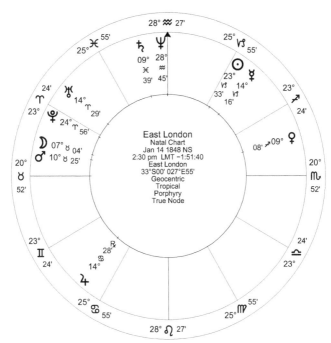

East London, 27E55, 33S00
January 14, 1848, 2:30 p.m. LMT
Source: Stadsbiblioteek

times, the most famous uprising occurred in June 1976 when the Soweto township erupted in rebellion (progressed ASC trine Mars). Johannesburg is also the home of the Apartheid Museum and the Museum of Africa. It's also the largest city in South Africa and the economic engine of the country. Goldfields abound just outside the downtown area.

Elevation: 5800 fcct

Incorporated: September 1928

Kimberley

When one thinks of this place, one thinks of diamonds. From the moment of the discovery of the most-valuable gem on earth until 1915, Kimberley was called the "diamond center of the world."

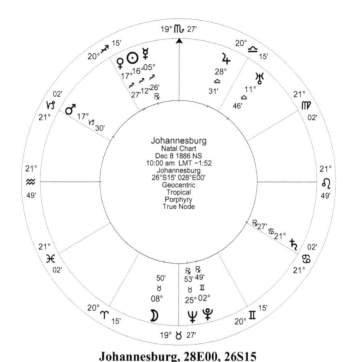

Johannesburg, 28E00, 26S15
December 8, 1886, 10:00 a.m. LMT
Sources: Standard Encyclopedia of South Africa says 10:00 a.m.

The "Big Hole" was an excavation about 1 mile in circumference and 4000 feet deep that yielded over 3 tons of diamonds and over 20 tons of earth.

A railroad to Cape Town was built in 1885 (progressed ASC sextile Mercury) and three years later, Cecil Rhodes founded DeBeers (progressed MC opposition Saturn) the premier diamond cartel in the world for many years.

In February 1900, the city endured a siege during the Boer War (progressed ASC square Uranus). The "Big Hole" or Kimberley mine closed in 1915 (progressed MC conjunct Mercury and ASC/MC midpoint).

Incorporated: 1912 (city)

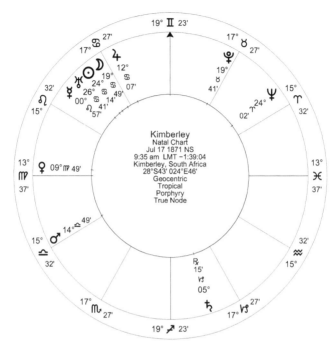

Kimberley, 24E46, 28S43
July 17, 1871, 9:35 a.m. LMT
Source: Public Library

Port Elizabeth

Port Elizabeth was founded in June 1820 and named. for the wife of the Cape Colony governor, Sir Rufane Donkin. A railroad to Kimberley (the diamond center) was completed in 1873 (progressed ASC opposition Mercury). The University of Port Elizabeth opened in 1964 (progressed MC trine Jupiter).

The city lies on Algoa Bay where the Baakens river meets the Indian Ocean.

Incorporated: 1861 (town), 1913 (city)

Pretoria

Pretoria is the administrative capital of South Africa, located on

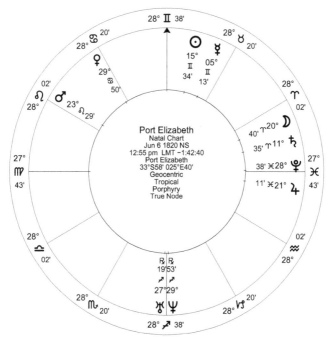

Port Elizabeth, 25E40, 33S58
June 6, 1820, 12:55 p.m. LMT
Source: Stadbiblioteek

the Apies river some 45 miles from Johannesburg. It was founded by Marthenius Pretorius in November 1855.

Pretoria was the capital of the Transvaal in 1860 (progressed MC conjunct Mercury) and the administrative capital of South Africa since May 1910 (progressed MC sextile Jupiter).

Railroads to both Cape Town and Durban were completed in 1893 (progressed MC sextile Venus) and a university opened in 1908 (progressed MC sextile Jupiter).

Pretoria was captured in 1899 during the early days of the Boer War (progressed MC square Mars and Neptune). That was ended with the signing of the Peace of Vereeniging in late May 1902 (progressed ASC semisquare Pluto).

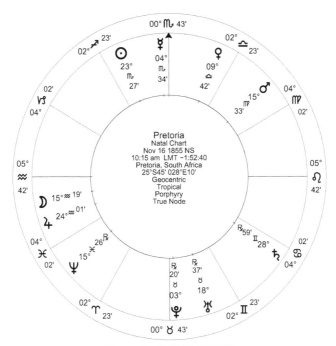

Pretoria, 25E40, 33S58
November 16, 1855, 10:15 a.m. LMT
Source: Standard Encyclopedia of South Africa

The main sights in Pretoria are Church Square and the nearby Paul Kruger House, the National Zoological Gardens and the Voortrekker monument.

Incorporated: October 1931 (city)

129

Sudan

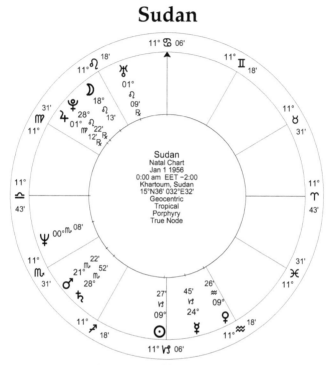

Khartoum, 32E32, 15N36
January 1, 1956, 12:00 a.m. EET
Source: *Los Angeles Times* and *New York Times*

Around 2000 B.C., this region was part of Egypt and called Nubia. A thousand years later, it was known as Kush. During the 6th century A.D., Christians arrived (Coptics) and the following century, Islam made its entrance. During the 1820s, Egypt seized control. The Mahdi took over from 1881 until 1885 when the Mahdi was killed as was General Gordon when Khartoum fell.

In September 1898 the British and Egyptians put down a rebellion at the Battle of Omdurman and by January 1899, Britain and Egypt agreed to rule the region jointly as the Anglo-Egyptian Condominium. Independence was achieved in January 1956.

In 1958, Ibrahim Abboud was elected and when he resigned in

1964 a civil was broke out (progressed Sun inconjunct Moon) between Moslems in the north and Christians in the south. The civil war ended in 1972 (progressed MC trine Saturn, progressed ASC sextile Pluto). Islamic (or sharia) law was established in 1983 by Nimieri (progressed MC inconjunct Sun opposition Venus, progressed ASC sextile Sun square Venus). President Nimieri was overthrown during a coup in April 1985 (progressed Sun square Venus) at which point another civil war erupted and a famine cost the lives of over two million. A coup broke out with Omar Bashir as leader in June 1989. In 1991, the US stopped relief efforts for seven million victims of the famine due to increasing political tensions (progressed MC conjunct Moon, progressed ASC square Moon).

In 1998, another famine broke out in the south (progressed MC sesquare Sun inconjunct Mercury) and by January 2002, a cease-fire ended the civil war (progressed MC conjunct Pluto). A rebellion in the Darfur region of western Sudan began in 2003. As of mid-2007, more than 300,000 have been killed and more than 2.5 million reported homeless have fled the region (progressed MC conjunct Pluto square Saturn, progressed ASC conjunct Saturn square Pluto, progressed Sun opposition Pluto). Some consider this a genocide to rid the region of dissident elements.

The Sudan is a country of 40 million people of whom 40 percent are Arab and 55 percent are Black. Over 70 percent are Moslem while only five percent are Christian.

The Sudan is the largest country in area in Africa (967,000 square miles) over four times the size of France, almost four times the size of Texas and six times the size of California. The northern part is grassland and savanna, the center has the Libyan and Nubian deserts while the south has rainforests. The Blue and the White Nile meet at Khartoum. The coastline along the Red Sea is 530 miles long. The main exports are cotton, gum arabic, sesame seeds and livestock.

Khartoum

Khartoum, the capital, was founded in 1821 as an army camp by Muhammad Ali at the junction of the Blue Nile and the White

Nile. Its name means "at the end of the elephant's trunk." The city was destroyed by the Mahdi in January 1885 when the British general, Charles "Chinese" Gordon was killed. The town of Omdurman then became the capital.

A new city of Khartoum was built in 1898 by General H. H. Kitchener. A University was founded in 1902 and by 1977, an oil pipeline was completed to Port Sudan. The present city consists of Khartoum proper, Khartoum North and Omdurman.

Swaziland

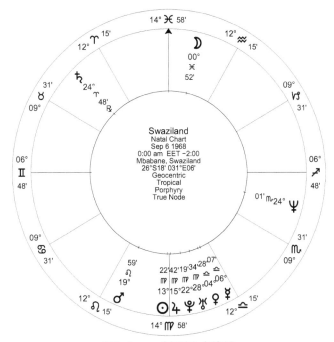

Mbabane, 31E06, 26S18
September 6, 1968, 12:00 a.m. EET
Source: *New York Times* and *London Times*

During the 18th century, the Bantus united to form the Swazi nation. In the 1820s, the Swazis were driven to this region by the Zulus and by the 1840s had asked for British protection from the Zulus. Gold was discovered in the 1880s. In November 1893, Swaziland was put under administration from the Transvaal and in December 1906 was put under direct British control. Independence came in September 1968.

The Constitution was suspended in 1973 and by 1976, King Sobhuza took over (progressed MC opposition Pluto, progressed ASC square Sun, progressed Sun conjunct Pluto) King Sobhuza died in 1982 after having ruled the kingdom for 82 years.

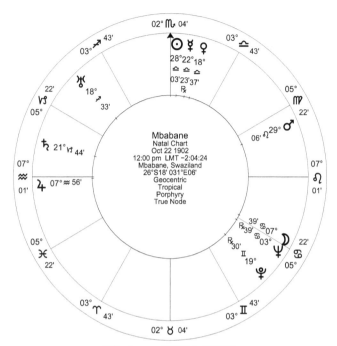

Mbabane, 31E06, 26S18
October 22, 1902, 12:00 p.m. LMT
Source: Embassy of Swaziland

Swaziland is a land of one million people living in an area about the size of New Jersey. The western region has the Highveld (up to 4000 feet high), the center has the Middleveld (up to 3000 feet high) and in the east is the Lowveld (about 1000 feet high). Much of Swaziland is meadowland and pastures. Main exports are farm products, sugar and cotton. About 40 percent of the adult population has AIDS.

Mbabane

Mbabane was founded as a trading station in 1869 and became the capital of Swaziland in October 1902. A railroad was built to Mozambique in 1964, and Mbabane became a city in April 1992.

Elevation: 3770 feet

Tanzania

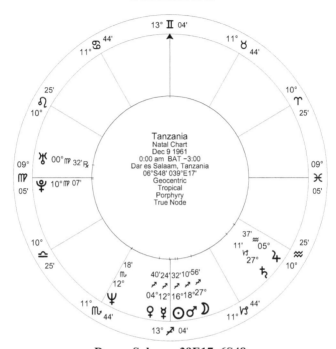

Dar es Salaam, 39E17, 6S48
December 9, 1961, 12:00 a.m. BGT
Sources: *London Times* **and** *New York Times*

In the 8th century A.D., Arab, Persian and Chinese traders plied the region. In the early 16th century, Portuguese traders had set up shop on both the mainland and the island of Zanzibar. The region came under Omani rule in 1652. In June 1890, the British took Zanzibar and Pemba under their wing and made them a Protectorate. The Germans occupied the mainland until after World War I, when the British took control in January 1920. Independence for the mainland section, called Tanganyika took place in December 1961. Zanzibar and Pemba came aboard in April 1964 to form the nation of Tanzania.

The first leader was Julius Nyerere, a socialist (progressed MC

135

opposition Sun, progressed ASC square Mercury sesquare Saturn sextile Neptune, progressed Sun conjunct Mars semisquare Jupiter). In 1979, Tanzania invaded Uganda to oust the infamous dictator, Idi Amin (progressed MC sextile Uranus). Nyerere stepped down in 1985 (progressed Sun trine Pluto). By December 1996, 500,000 Hutus fleeing Rwanda had left Tanzania and returned home (progressed MC inconjunct Mars).

Tanzania is a country of 38 million people living in an area three times the size of Arizona or twice the area of Spain. The mainland was once called Tanganyika but the country also has the islands of Zanzibar (640 square miles) and Pemba (380 square miles). From the narrow coastal plain, the land rises to a 5000 foot plateau of grassland and savanna. The Great Rift Valley is the prominent geographical feature and has produced Lakes Victoria, Nyasa (Malawi) and Tanganyika, which is 400 miles long and the biggest lake in Africa. The highest point is Mt. Kilimanjaro (elev. 19,340 ft.), the highest point on the continent. The coastline is 885 miles long. The main exports are coffee, cotton, tobacco, cashews, sisal and cloves from Zanzibar. About 10 percent of the adult population has AIDS.

Dar es Salaam

Dar es Salaam was founded in 1862 by the Sultan of Zanzibar. The German East Africa Co. arrived in 1885 and it became the capital of German East Africa from 1891 until 1916 when the British took over. The university was founded in 1961.

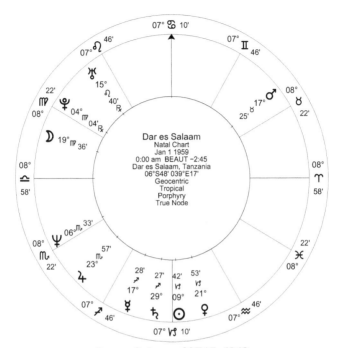

Dar es Salaam, 39E17, 6S48
January 1, 1949 at 12:00 a.m.
Source: Tanzania Library Service

Togo

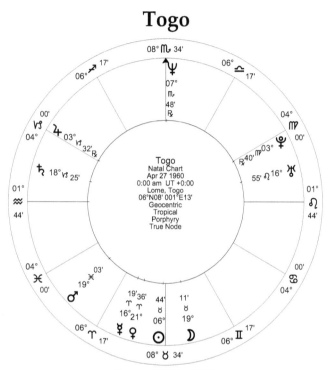

Lome, 1E13, 6N08
April 27, 1960, 12:00 a.m. GMT
Source: *New York Times*

Portuguese explorers reached the region during the 15th century. During the 17th-19th centuries, Togo was part of the slave coast. In July 1884, the area became a German colony. After World War I Britain took the western third of the territory while France took the remainder. In 1956, the British sector joined Ghana.

When Togo became independent in April 1960, Sylvanus Olympio became its first leader. He was assassinated in January 1963 and Grunitzsky took over the reins of power (progressed ASC semisquare Mars inconjunct Pluto). The Constitution was suspended in 1967 when Eyadema became President (progressed

138

MC inconjunct Mercury). Eyadema died in February 2005 (progressed MC trine Venus semisquare Neptune, progressed ASC sextile Moon conjunct Mars semisquare Sun, progressed Sun square Mars).

Togo is a country of 5.5 million people living in an area the size of West Virginia or Croatia. The 35 mile coastline is sandy. Small mountains and savanna occupy the interior. Main exports are cocoa, coffee and cotton.

Lome

Lome, the capital, was founded in the 18th century on the Gulf of Guinea and originally known as Bay Beach. Lome became the capital of German Togoland in 1897. The university was founded in 1965.

Tunisia

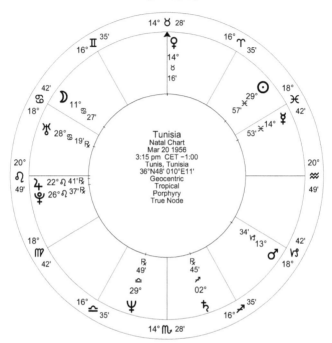

March 20, 1956, 3:15 p.m. CET
Tunis, 36N48, 10E11
Source: My rectification

The Phoenicians arrived in the region around 1000 B.C. and by 814 B.C., they had founded the city of Carthage. The Romans destroyed the city in 146 B.C.: they ruled Tunisia until 429 A.D. The Byzantine Empire invaded in the 6th century but were driven out by the Arabs who came in 670 A.D. bringing Islam with them.

In 1574, Tunisia became part of the vast Ottoman Empire and the French occupied the region after May 1881. During World War II, Tunisia was under Vichy rule. The French signed a Protocol on March 20, 1956 in Paris agreeing to end the protectorate and pull out its troops. Celebrations began that night in the capital celebrating this move.

For the same reasons given in the section on Morocco, I don't find that the transits or progressions using the chart in Nicholas Campion's book work for me. He uses the date of June 15, 1956, and the time of 5:00 p.m. My own rectification and newspaper reports seem to indicate the time I've chosen.

The Monarchy was thrown out and a Republic proclaimed in July 1957 (progressed MC sextile Mercury, progressed ASC square Jupiter). Socialism was introduced in 1959 (progressed Sun trine Saturn) and Tunisia nationalized its assets in 1964 (progressed MC square Jupiter, progressed ASC square Pluto semisquare Moon, progressed Sun sesquare Jupiter).

The long-ruling President Habib Bourguiba was ousted in 1987 (progressed MC square Mercury, progressed Sun semisquare Mercury). A rebellion broke out in October 1994 (progressed MC sextile Jupiter) and Islamic militants set off bombs in April 2002 (progressed MC square Sun semisquare Venus, progressed ASC opposition Sun, progressed Sun sextile Mercury).

Tunis

Tunis lies on the west bank of the Lac de Tunis lagoon some six miles from the Mediterranean Sea. Much of Tunis lies on the ruins of Carthage, which was founded about 814 B.C. The Romans arrived in 146 B.C. and the Arabs came in the 7th century A.D. Ottoman occupation began in 1539 and lasted until the 19th century. A university was founded in 1960.

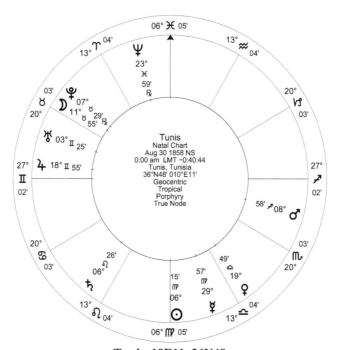

Tunis, 10E11, 36N48
August 30, 1858, l2:00 a.m. LMT
Source: Municipalite de Tunis

Uganda

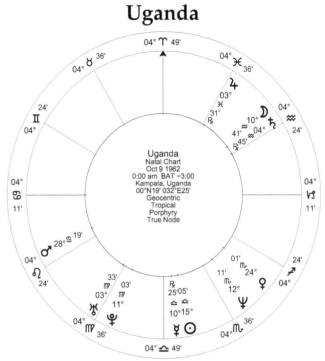

Kampala, 32E25, 0N19
October 9, 1962, l2:00 a.m. BGT
Source: *London Times*

During the 19th century, this region was known as the Kingdom of Buganda. Arabs seized control in 1830 but by 1890, the British held sway. Uganda became a British Protectorate in June 1894. During World War I, naval battles Britain and Germany took place on Lake Victoria. Independence came in October 1962.

Milton Obote abolished the kingdoms in 1967 (progressed MC sextile Moon opposition Mercury sesquare Venus, progressed ASC sesquare Venus). Obote was ousted from power by Idi Amin in January 1971 (progressed ASC square Mercury). He forced the Asians out of the country the following year (progressed MC opposition Sun, progressed ASC trine Neptune sextile Pluto, progressed Sun semisquare Pluto). A border dispute with Tanzania erupted in 1978 (progressed ASC semisquare Uranus sesquare Pluto) and Tanzania invaded Uganda in April 1979 to overthrow Amin. During Idi Amin's reign of terror, over 300,000 were killed. Obote again took the reins of power but he too was ousted in July 1985 (progressed MC square Mars sesquare Pluto, progressed ASC trine Venus).

The kingdoms were restored in July 1993 bringing a good deal of stability to the country, even though the kings had little real power and their presence was little more than symbolic. A rebellion in the north erupted in 2002, more than two million fled the country and more than 100,000 were killed (progressed MC inconjunct Sun, progressed ASC opposition Moon sextile Mercury, progressed Sun semisquare Mercury conjunct Venus).

Uganda is a country of 28 million people living in an area the size of Oregon or Romania. Its southern border is Lake Victoria, source of the Nile River. In the west is the Great Rift Valley and Lakes Albert and Edward. The center consists of a wooded savanna and in the southwest are volcanoes. The highest point is Mt. Ruwenzori (elev. 16,765 ft.) The main exports are coffee, gold and fish.

Kampala

Kampala was founded in December 1890 on the site of Mengo where the King of Buganda had his palace. It was built on four hills by Capt. Lugard. A university was established in 1922.

During the infamous reign of Idi Amin, the Israelis invaded the airport at Entebbe trying to free hostages on an airliner (progressed MC conjunct Mars, progressed ASC conjunct Pluto). Uganda was invaded by forces from neighboring Tanzania in 1979 putting an end to Amin's dictatorial regime (progressed MC square Venus, Neptune and Pluto).

Elevation: 3900 feet

Incorporated: 1949

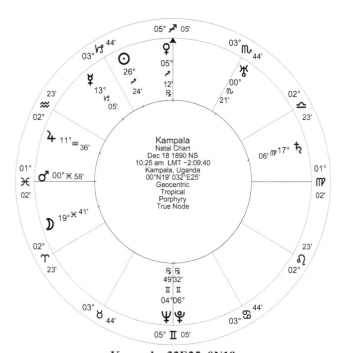

Kampala, 32E25, 0N19
December 18, 1890, 10:25 a.m. LMT
Source: Encyclopedia Britannica

Zaire

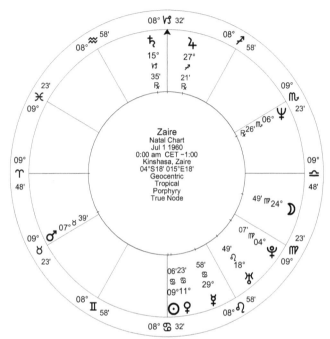

Kinshasa, 15E18, 4S18
July 1, 1960, 12:00 a.m. MET
Source: *London Times*

In ancient times. this region was part of the Bantu Kingdoms of Kongo. Luba and Lunda. Portuguese navigators reached the mouth of the Congo in 1482 but settlement was sparse. Henry Morton Stanley began to explore this vast region in 1876 and by 1885. the area became the personal property of the King of the Belgians called the Congo Free State. In October 1908. it became a colony of Belgium. The atrocities committed during this time were a precursor to the turmoil that occurred after independence came in late June 1960.

The provinces of Katanga and Kasai immediately proclaimed their own independence. Joseph Kasabuvu became president and

Patrice Lumumba became the prime minister. Mobutu Sese Seko took over in November 1960 and Lumumba was murdered in January 1961 (progressed MC opposition Sun, progressed ASC square Sun/Venus, progressed Sun conjunct Sun/Venus). Moise Tshombe became president in June 1964 (progressed MC opposition Venus) at the same time that UN troops left the region. A rebellion in the Stanleyville region ended in July 1965 after nine months of conflict (progressed Sun opposition Saturn). The country was renamed Zaire in 1971 (progressed MC sesquare Pluto, progressed Sun semisquare Pluto).

By 1977, a new rebellion had broken out in the Katanga province (progressed MC trine Moon, progressed Sun sextile Moon). Mobutu ended a ban on political parties in 1990 (progressed MC square Neptune, progressed ASC sextile Venus sesquare Jupiter, progressed Sun square Mars). Refugees from the civil war in neighboring Rwanda flooded into Zaire in 1994 (progressed MC sesquare Moon inconjunct Venus, progressed ASC trine Saturn, progressed Sun semisquare Moon). Two years later, ethnic violence erupted in the refugee camps (progressed MC semisquare Jupiter, progressed Sun sesquare Jupiter).

Mobutu died while in exile in September 1997 and Kabila took over (progressed ASC square Uranus, progressed Sun inconjunct Saturn). Kabila was assassinated in January 2001 after 3.5 million had died in the civil war (progressed MC opposition Uranus, progressed Sun conjunct Uranus).

Zaire is a country of 60 million people living in an area three times the size of Turkey or more than three times the area of Texas. It's the third-largest country in Africa in area. Straddling the Equator, the north is a dense rainforest, in the center are grasslands and in the south is the savanna. Zaire is home to the Congo River basin. The east has very high mountains and is part of the Great Rift Valley where Lakes Albert, Edward, Kivu and Tanganyika are located. Zaire has only a 23 mile long coastline and the highest point is Mt. Ruwenzori (elev. 16,765 ft.) on the border with Uganda. The main exports are diamonds, copper, coffee and cobalt.

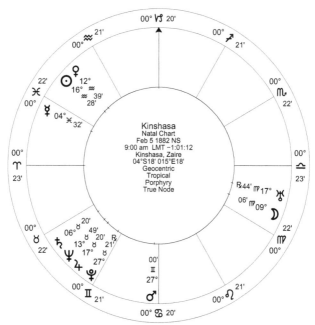

Kinshasa, 15E18, 4S18
February 5, 1882 at 9:00 a.m. LMT
Source: Embassy of Zaire

Kinshasa

In 1877, Henry Morton Stanley arrived at this point which was inhabited as Kintambo and Kinshasa. A new city was begun in late 1881 and formally dedicated in February 1882. It was called Leopoldville after the King of Belgium. A railroad was completed in 1898 to the port of Matadi (progressed MC opposition Jupiter/Uranus). A pipeline was opened to Matadi in 1914 (progressed ASC sextile Moon). Air service to Stanleyville began in 1920 and Leopoldville/Kinshasa became the capital of the Belgian Congo in 1923 (progressed MC opposition Venus, progressed ASC opposition Jupiter).

Pre-independence rioting began in January 1959 (progressed MC conjunct Uranus) and the city's name was formally changed in June 1966 (progressed ASC opposition Mars).

148

Zambia

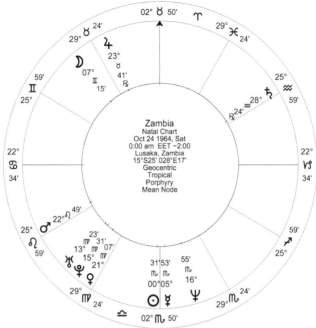

Lusaka, 28E17, 15S25
October 24, 1964, 12:00 a.m. EET
Sources: *London Times* and *New York Times*

Between the 15th and 19th centuries, the Bantus made this their home. In November 1855, David Livingstone explored the region and discovered Victoria Falls. Cecil Rhodes and his South Africa Co. arrived in October 1899 and in August 1911, the region was named for him as Northern Rhodesia. Direct colonial rule started in April 1924. The Federation of Northern and South Rhodesia and Nyasaland was formed in 1953, but it fell apart ten years later when independence came in October 1964. Kenneth Kaunda became President until 1991.

The copper mines were taken over by the government in 1970 (progressed ASC inconjunct Saturn semisquare Uranus, progressed Sun conjunct Mercury semisquare Venus). More firms and companies were nationalized in 1975 (progressed MC trine Uranus, progressed ASC square Sun/Mercury). Food riots erupted in June 1990 as the price of maize and other basic foodstuffs doubled (progressed MC square Saturn). A failed coup by former President Kaunda who had been out of office for six years and was highly critical of the new government broke out in October 1997 (progressed conjunct Moon inconjunct Mercury, progressed ASC opposition Saturn). Former President Chiluba was arrested on embezzlement charges in February 2003.

Zambia is a country of 12 million people living in an area twice the size of Montana or the size of Turkey. It lies on a forested plateau with mountains in the northeast. The southern tier is part of the Zambezi river basin. The main exports are copper (world's number five), cobalt (world's number two), lead and zinc. About 15 percent of the adult population has AIDS.

Lusaka

The first settlement in the region was founded to serve the lead mine at Kabwe. Lusaka was formally founded in late July 1913 and became the capital of Northern Rhodesia in 1935 (progressed MC conjunct Moon, progressed ASC square Jupiter). The University of Zambia was founded in 1965.

Elevation: 4200 feet

Incorporated: September 1960

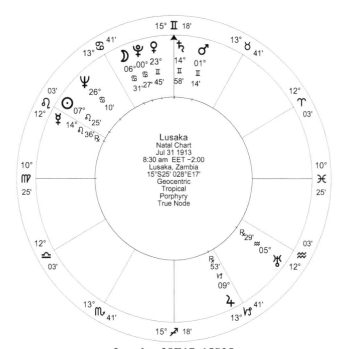

Lusaka, 28E17, 15S25
July 31, 1913, 8:30 a.m. EET
Source: City Library

151

Zimbabwe

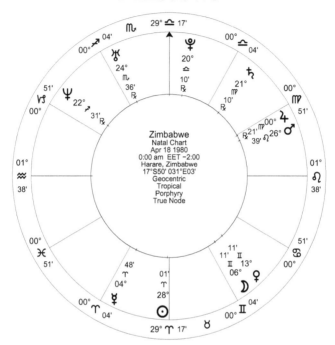

Harare, 31E03, 17S50
April 18, 1980, 12:00 a.m. EET
Source: *London Times* and *San Francisco Examiner*

Around 1000 A.D., the Shona culture was dominant. They built a city called Zimbabwe, for which the present country is named. The Bantus arrived in the 15th century and Portuguese slave traders plied the region from the 16th to 19th centuries. In October 1889, Cecil Rhodes and his South Africa Co. arrived and the region became Rhodesia which was governed by his company. The region was partitioned in September 1923 and made a British Crown Colony. It was a self-governing state ruled by whites. In 1961, a new Constitution guaranteed the continuation of white rule.

Meanwhile, in October 1953, the region entered into a Federation with Northern Rhodesia and Nyasaland that lasted until January 1964, The leader of Southern Rhodesia, Ian Smith, declared independence in November 1965 but Britain refused to accept it. In May 1968, UN sanctions and a trade embargo emerged. Another Constitution in 1970 barred all blacks from the political scene. Elections were held in April 1979 and by December that year, a cease-fire with the Patriotic Front was signed.

Independence with British approval was granted in April 1980 with Robert Mugabe as President. The country was also renamed. Mugabe was a Socialist or Marxist whose policies almost brought the country to the edge of ruin. He renounced Marxism in 1991. In February 2000, a fuel crisis erupted in the midst of 60 percent inflation and 50 percent unemployment. Mugabe rejected the new Constitution and seized farms owned by whites without compensation (progressed MC sesquare Mercury, progressed ASC semisquare Mercury). He continues to rant his invectives against practically everyone, including homosexuals and other people he considers undesirable. Meanwhile, 25 percent of the country has AIDS and is in dire economic straits.

At the beginning of 2008, this is a country fast approaching calamity. In 2007, the inflation rate was 1730 percent; in 2008, it's over 100,000 percent, considerable worse than Weimar Germany after World War I. More than 80 percent of the people are unemployed and 70 percent of those between 18 and 60 have left the country seeking work elsewhere. Life expectancy has dropped to 34 for women and 37 for men. It's all the fault of Mugabe, who at 84 is trying to hold onto power while his country goes down the tubes. An election at the end of March 2008 was probably rigged event hough the preliminary tally showed Mugabe losing. He seems to have a death wish for his country (progressed MC square Mars, progressed ASC opposition Mars).

Mugabe finally agreed to share power with Morgan Tsvangirai who literally won the March election, but Mugabe refused to concede. Meanwhile, the inflation rate had escalated to more than 11 million percent. Whoever takes the helm will have a difficult task getting the country back on track.

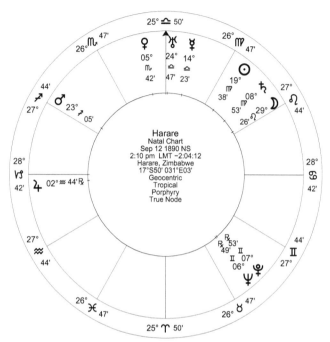

Harare, 31E03, 17S50
September 12, 1890, 2:10 p.m. LMT
Source: Public Library

Zimbabwe has 13 million people in an area the size of California or Germany. It lies on a high plateau between the Zambezi and Limpopo rivers. A high veldt runs northeast to southwest. The main exports are asbestos (world's number four) and chromium (world's number six).

Harare

This city was founded in September 1890 at the spot where the Pioneer Column stopped on its march to Mashonaland and named Salisbury for the British Prime Minister. A railroad was opened to Beira in 1899 (progressed MC conjunct Venus). The University of Southern Rhodesia was founded in 1957 (ASC sextile Jupiter). Guerrillas attacked the city in July 1978 (progressed MC square Uranus, progressed ASC trine Mars) shortly before the city changed

154

its name to Harare and the country changed its name to Zimbabwe. Harare today is one of the world's largest tobacco markets.

Elevation: 4865 feet

Incorporated: 1897 (municipality), 1935 (city)

Birth Data for Famous African Personalities

Algeria

Houari Boumedienne, August 23, 1932, Heliopolis, Algeria

Cental African Republic

Jean Bedel Bokassa, February 22, 1921, Bobangui, C.A.R.

David Dacko, March 24, 1930, Bouchia, C.A.R.

Cote D'Ivoire

Houphouet-Boigny, October 18, 1905

Egypt

King Farouk, February 11, 1920, Cairo, Egypt, 10:30 p.m. per *Sabian Symbols*

Hosni Mubarak, May 4, 1928, Kafr el Meselha

Muhammad Naguib, February 20, 1901, Khartoum, Sudan

Gamal Abdul Nasser, January 15, 1918, Beni Mar, Egypt, 11:00 a.m. per Marion Meyer Drew or 4:00 a.m. per Edward Lyndoe

Anwar Sadat, December 25, 1918, Mit abu el Kom, Egypt, 12:20 a.m. per a report from the Embassy that he was born "shortly after midnight." Sadat said, "between midnight and 4:00 a.m."

Equitorial Guinea

Macian Nguema, January 1, 1924

Ethiopia

Haile Selassie, July 23, 1891, Ejarsa Gora, Ethiopia, 11:15 a.m. per *Sabian Symbols*

Ghana

Kwame Nkrumah, September 21, 1909, Nkroful, Ghana

Kenya

Daniel Arap Moi, September 2, 1924, Kuriengwo, Kenya

Jomo Kenyatta, October 20, 1894, Gatundu, Kenya

Liberia

Samuel Doe, May 6, 1951, Tuzon, Liberia

Charles Taylor, January 28, 1948

William Tolbert, May 13, 1913

William Tubman, November 29, 1895, Harper, Liberia

Libya

Moammar Qaddafi, September or October 1942, Sirte, Libya

Malawi

Hastings Banda, November 25, 1896 or 1897

Morocco

Hassasn II, July 9, 1929, Rabat, Morocco

Mohamed V, August 10, 1909, Rabat, Morocco

Mohamed VI, August 21, 1963, Rabat, Morocco

Nigeria

Sani Abacha, September 20, 1943, Kano, Nigeria

Yakubu Gowon, October 19, 1934, Lur, Nigeria

Senegal

Leopold Senghor, October 9, 1906, Joal, Senegal

Somalia

Mohamed Aidid, December 15, 1934, Mudug, Somalia

South Africa

F.W. de Klark, March 18, 1936, Johannesburg, South Africa, 11:30 p.m. per his mother who says "11:00 p.m. to midnight"

Paul Kruger, October 10, 1825, Colesburg, South Africa, 6:00 a.m. per *Notable Nativities*

Nelson Mandela, July 18, 1918, Umtata, South Africa, 3:00 p.m. per him "middle of the afternoon"

Cecil Rhodes, July 5, 1853, Bishop's Stortford, South Africa, 7:00 p.m. per *Sabian Symbols*

Jan Smuta, May 24, 1870, Riebeeck West, South Africa, 4:45 a.m. per *Sabian Symbols*

Tanzania

Julius Nyerere, April 13, 1922, Butiama, Tanzania

Togo

Gnassingbe Eyadema, December 26, 1937, Pya, Togo

Tunisia

Habib Bourguiba, August 3, 1903, Monastir, Tunisia

Sudan

Charles "Chinese" Gordon, January 28, 1833, Woolwich, England, 9:53 a.m. per the family Bible

Uganda

Idi Amin, mid-1920s, Kokobo, Uganda

Milton Obote, December 28, 1925, Apac, Uganda

Zaire

King Leopold II, April 9, 1835, Brussels, Belgium, 5:00 p.m. per *Sabian Symbols*

Patrice Lumumba, July 2, 1925, Onalua, Zaire

Mobutu Sese Seko, October 14, 1930, Lisala, Zaire

Moise Tshombe, October 10, 1919, Musumba, Zaire

Zambia

Kenneth Kaunda, April 28, 1924, Chincali, Zimbabwe

Zimbabwe

Robert Mugabe, February 21, 1924, Kutana, Zimbabwe

Other

Sir Richard Burton, March 19, 1821, Torquay, England, 9:30 p.m. per *Sabian Symbols* and *Notable Nativities*

David Livingstone, March 19, 1813, Blantyre, Scotland

Henry Morton Stanley, January 28, 1841, Denbigh, Wales, 5:30 a.m. per *Notable Nativities*

Bibliography

General Reference
    Britannica Almanac
    Information Please Almanac
    New York Times Almanac
    TIMES Almanac
    World Almanac
    Dunlop Encyclopedia of Facts
    Portable World Factbook by Kenneth Lye
    Reader's Digest to Places of the World
LIFE Library
    The Arab World
    South Africa
    Tropical Africa
Astrological Works
    Book of World Horoscopes by Nicholas Campion
    Mundane Astrology by Baigent, Campion and Harvey